Pasha

Pasha

MY STORY

PASHA KOVALEV

JOHN BLAKE

Published by John Blake Publishing Ltd,
3 Bramber Court, 2 Bramber Road,
London W14 9PB, England

www.johnblakebooks.com

www.facebook.com/johnblakebooks 🇫
twitter.com/jblakebooks 🇪

First published in hardback in 2013
This edition published in paperback in 2015

ISBN: 978 1 78418 001 0

British Library Cataloguing-in-Publication Data:

A catalogue record for this book is available from the British Library.

Design by www.envydesign.co.uk

Printed in Great Britain by CPI Group (UK) Ltd

1 3 5 7 9 10 8 6 4 2

Papers used by John Blake Publishing are natural, recyclable products made
from wood grown in sustainable forests. The manufacturing processes conform
to the environmental regulations of the country of origin.

Every attempt has been made to contact the relevant copyright-holders,
but some were unobtainable. We would be grateful if the appropriate
people could contact us.

CONTENTS

ACKNOWLEDGEMENTS

I believe it's the custom to dedicate a page of your autobiography to acknowledging all the people who assisted in bringing the book into existence.

This is my life story. There isn't one person I've encountered who hasn't influenced or shaped the course of my life in some way, however little. Without any of those people, this book would not be as it is. It wouldn't have been what you are about to read.

I cannot thank one person without thanking them all and if I did that then this book would simply be a seemingly endless list of names.

So thank you to everyone who has ever inspired me, advised me or shaped my path in any way, whether you did so knowingly or not. Thank you to all the people who have followed and supported my career. Thanks to all the people who followed my journey, whether on television or at one of the live shows.

Most of all, thank you to the people who stood back and gave me the freedom to do whatever I wanted and loved – the people who didn't try to influence me to do anything else but made me happy. It turned out that what made me happy was simply to dance and now I get to do that every day I am alive. I remain humble and grateful for that amazing opportunity.

Pasha

FOREWORD

The thing about Pasha Kovalev is that he's absolutely incapable of doing or saying anything that might be described as 'self-promotion'. Despite being one of the most talented dancers in the industry, handsome and charming to boot, he never, ever boasts. So I think what I'm going to have to do in this foreword is all of Pasha's boasting for him! I think it's important that you really understand how special the man whose story you're about to read is.

People often strike up a conversation with me about my experience as a contestant on *Strictly Come Dancing* and it quickly becomes apparent that they're not interested in me in the slightest – everyone wants to know about Pasha! The most common question is: 'Is Pasha as lovely as he appears on television?'

To everyone who has ever pondered that question, I have to tell you that the answer is a resounding 'yes'! Pasha finds a level with everyone he meets. Spending so much time together for *Strictly*, I observed the way he was with people – men, women and children – and he'd always find a way to make them feel uniquely cherished. It doesn't matter where you come from or what you do, Pasha finds a way to make you feel like you're the centre of the universe. He weaves a quiet magic that leaves everyone he encounters eager to spend more time with him.

Pasha is universally popular with everyone that he meets and his charisma shines out through the television screen and radiates out from a stage. But he doesn't crave approval or try to be admired and, ironically, that's exactly why he is.

Despite being under immense pressure to teach me the incredibly complicated and skilful art of ballroom dancing over a period of just weeks, Pasha never once lost his cool. I have never seen his equilibrium slip. Within our working relationship, he was always the calm and I was the storm. If I was freaking out one week about what comments the *Strictly* judges might make about our routine, for example, he'd always know what to say or do to reassure me. Invariably, he'd say, 'Why would you ever worry about that? Just focus on the dance.'

I think Pasha's advice to me in those situations reflects his general philosophy on life. All the fame and adoration he has now has happened by accident rather than design. But, ultimately, while he loves engaging with his fans and is very grateful for their support, he is first and foremost completely devoted to his craft. He isn't afraid of hard graft in order to be the very best dancer he can possibly be. He's always striving to improve, too. This is without question reflected in his performance – his technical ability is astounding.

Having said that, though, Pasha's number-one priority when dancing is to make his partner look good. When I partnered him on *Strictly*, he was there being quietly brilliant in the background in a way that allowed me to shine. I see him doing that with every person he partners. Other dancers want all eyes to be on them, but not Pasha; he is a phenomenal teacher and he knew how to bring out the best in me.

Pasha wouldn't have been able to teach me to ballroom dance the way he did if I hadn't trusted him. My trust was something he was able to gain with ease. I was never worried that we were doing anything that would leave me feeling humiliated, simply to generate a headline. He gets genuine pleasure from seeing other people fulfil their potential.

What surprised me most about meeting and working with Pasha was his sense of humour. Russians have a reputation for being quite solemn, but he managed to have me in hysterics a lot of the time. Although Pasha originates from Russia, and is now an American citizen, I feel that his humour is very British in its nature. He is very dry and super-quick to make a witty remark, even though English is his second language.

Pasha and I found common ground when working together in that we are both our own harshest critics. This can sometimes be a good trait – it means that you're constantly striving to improve your skill – but it can also mean that you don't take the time to enjoy your achievements and pat yourself on the back. While you're reading this book, remember that, every time Pasha says he was 'lucky' to get an opportunity, it means that he worked hours beyond human endurance to showcase his talent and get that chance. Every time he says that he performed 'well', you should read 'fantastic'. Exaggerate everything Pasha writes by a factor of ten, don't let his humility fool you and you'll really get a sense of how extraordinary he is.

There aren't many of Pasha's kind left in the world; he is a true gentleman. What strikes you most about him, though, is his quiet confidence. In an industry that's notoriously full of huge egos masking even bigger insecurities, I've never seen Pasha have a moment of self-consciousness.

You can guarantee that you won't find salacious bits of celebrity tittle-tattle within the pages of this book. What you *will* find is the extraordinary story of a man who danced his way from the unlikeliest of roots to become a national treasure.

I hope that you will find reading Pasha's journey as inspiring as I found it to work with him.

Enjoy!

Kimberley Walsh
2013

PREFACE

It's Saturday, 29 November 2014. BBC1's *Strictly Come Dancing* is kicking primetime rival *The X Factor*'s proverbial butt in the viewing figure ratings wars, and it's big news in the tabloid press. That's how I know that approximately ten million people have just watched my friend Pasha Kovalev and his celebrity dance partner, Caroline Flack, perform an impressive, high-energy Charleston set in an imaginary Moroccan spice market.

The routine has inspired a standing ovation from the live studio audience, and I can already tell from the way notoriously hard-to-impress judge Craig Revel Horwood has sat up just a fraction straighter (I'm sitting just to his right, close enough to smell him – he smells nice) that Pasha and Caroline are going to get a high score. It's a crucial stage in the competition and, in retrospect, this will be the performance that marks Pasha and

Caroline out as the couple who ultimately lift the coveted Glitterball trophy and emerge as victors of the 2014 series.

Yet instead of basking in his moment of triumph, I see Pasha's eyes scan the crowd for me. When we catch each other's glance he mouths, 'Can you see okay?' By way of response, I nod vigorously and give a rather gawky 'thumbs up' to indicate that I'm having a jolly old time (I'm not especially known for my coolness). The judges deliver their unanimous positive verdicts on Pasha and Caroline's performance and with a brief, barely perceptible wink in my direction, they go dashing up the famous, post-routine staircase, where co-host Claudia Winkleman is waiting to give them a (rather sweaty, I imagine) embrace.

If you ever wanted to know what Pasha Kovalev is like in 'real life', the above anecdote pretty much sums him up. He's the sort of man concerned with whether his friend has a good view, even when you'd imagine his attentions would be entirely concentrated elsewhere. Indeed, he's the sort of man who, eighteen months previously, had turned up on my doorstep for our very first meeting with two huge bottles of cloudy apple juice, having texted me beforehand to ask me what I most liked to drink whilst writing (I nobly resisted the urge to say 'wine'). In short, Pasha is a diamond. And as someone whose work involves keeping one metaphorical foot in the world of media and celebrity, I know him to be a rare diamond, completely unaffected by his status as heartthrob/reigning *Strictly* champion and one of the country's most beloved TV stars.

Apple Juice Day (as it shall henceforth be known) marked the beginning of our time writing the original, hardback incarnation of this book. Pasha would arrive at my flat in East

London, always removing his shoes at the door before flopping down into one of my big, squishy armchairs (invariably exhausted from having spent the requisite ten hours per day rehearsing) and telling me about his life. I'd diligently scribble his words on an A4 jotter until his mouth, my hand and both of our brains ached.

I learned many things from Pasha and his life experiences. I learned that Siberia isn't cold all year round (who knew?). I learned that communism isn't the brilliant, utopian-style idea I'd originally imagined it was. I learned the true extent of the physical and mental dedication it takes to dance with the flair and precision that he does. I also learned that, as long as you remain super-active, it's entirely possible to eat your own bodyweight in chocolate every day and not gain an ounce.

Together, Pasha and I documented his early childhood, which he spent using his well-developed imagination to turn his stark, grey, Siberian hometown into a magical wonderland, fit for fantasy adventures. He described how he came to fall deeply and irrevocably in love with ballroom dancing as a seven-year-old. This led to an ambition to pursue dance as a career, no matter what the sacrifice – no matter how many hours were spent travelling through Siberia on a freezing-cold bus during the winter months, or how many miles he had to move away from his family home with his dance school. It ultimately shaped everything that was to come. I learned that Pasha never actively sought fame and that he is impressively single-minded in his dogged pursuit of dual goals: to dance to the best of his ability, and to teach other people to dance to the best of theirs. It is these goals which ultimately led him into television – a decision he initially approached with trepidation.

All of this you will discover as you read the pages that follow, but it's worth foregrounding it, because it's this central paradox which makes Pasha and his story so fascinating. He is, in some ways, the epitome of showbiz: the show must always go on, even if he's cracked a rib. He loves colour and sequins and entertaining a crowd. Yet he's unlike any other famous person I've ever known, literally incapable of becoming high-maintenance.

I will admit to knowing relatively little about *Strictly Come Dancing* before becoming friends with Pasha. (I'm an avid fan now and can often be found exchanging frenzied tweets with fellow Pasha admirer Marian Keyes on a Saturday night during the autumn months.) Up until that point, I'd caught the odd show and knew it had something to do with celebs, glitter and Len Goodman being a legend with his one-liners. I assumed that Pasha would come cha-cha-cha-ing into my life, adorned in multiple feather boas and demanding I furnish him with a foam-free soya mocha choca decaf latte and six white kittens dyed pink before we could commence the writing process. As it was, he caught the tube to my gaff (the story you'll read later about walking from the tube station and meeting a canine fan relates to one of his many visits chez Devon), waited to be offered a beverage and opted for a super low-maintenance cup of tea (no kittens, pink or otherwise).

Having established that we were pretty comfortable in each other's company, he then told me he'd spent the day attempting to dance with comedian Miranda Hart – who was at the time on crutches following an injury, and is over six feet tall – for 'That thing you have in the UK where you put on noses for fun and charity' (Comic Relief). I can't explain why, but something about the way he told me that story made me sure we'd remain friends after the book had been written. It might have been because I said, 'How are you?' and he'd replied 'Very tired,' and gone on to qualify that statement with the Miranda anecdote. It struck me as being refreshingly honest but without meandering into whinging territory.

And that's another important thing to know about Pasha – he hardly ever complains and he *never* exaggerates. At first, as his writing partner, I found this challenging. I am used to asking my interviewees, 'And how did that make you feel?' In response to which they give me a verbose account of the emotional rollercoaster which defined their state throughout every nanosecond of whatever situation we're documenting.

So when I asked Pasha how he felt about certain tough incidents throughout his life and he replied in his trademark transatlantic drawl, 'Well, you know, it is what it is,' I initially mistook his extreme laidback-ness for a reluctance to open up. What I soon discovered – and what you will discover too, as a reader – is that Pasha is philosophical to the point of stoicism about absolutely everything, and that is part of what makes him marvellous. I'd go so far as to say his attitude is inspiring, especially if you're someone with a propensity for 'sweating the small stuff'.

Pasha recounts his memories with a balance and truthfulness that's rare in everyday conversation, and even rarer when affording someone the opportunity to tell their life story without anyone to challenge their version of events. There is something raw and honest in the way he speaks of his memories, but it's never unnecessarily dramatic. It was from working with Pasha that I discovered 'having star quality' and 'talking loudly and incessantly' are not synonymous. Pasha is never trying to be the centre of attention, but invariably is anyway because he is the calm in the eye of the storm that is so often happening all around him.

I've never seen Pasha stressed. When I came to watch his touring stage show with Katya Virshilas in 2013, I met the four-strong cast at Katya's flat and we all got a lift up to the theatre together. Pasha was driving the huge, 4x4, tour-bus-style monstrosity we were travelling in and was running very late, caught up in what we Londoners refer to as 'nightmare traffic' (even though no one has ever woken in a cold sweat from a dream about tailgating on the M4). I thought Pasha's sense of professional obligation would at least give him mild road rage, but he was as tranquil as ever and, of course, we got there in plenty of time, largely because of him remaining so calm. (There was even enough time before the show for Pasha and Katya's physiotherapist, Colin, to fix my right ankle which had been giving me jip – something he did in approximately three seconds flat, because he is an actual genius).

That night, when I watched Pasha dance live for the first time, it marked the point when I felt I really 'got' who he was. We were about two-thirds of the way through writing the book at that stage and I'd already watched countless YouTube videos of his performances – but this was an entirely different experience.

Pasha had described so vividly the mechanics and the artistry of dancing that I felt I already knew what it would be like to see it in three dimensions. I was wrong. Knowing as I did (and as you will, soon) the history behind the performances, the blood, sweat and tears poured into creating the spectacle, magnified and enhanced the experience of being an audience member.

Performing is so much a part of who Pasha is. We might have spent days and days holed up in my little flat, ordering endless cartons of sushi and unravelling his early, formative experiences in a way that made me feel vaguely like a therapist, but I can honestly say it was during that live show that my understanding finally clicked into place. In the cab home I cried. It was impossible to say precisely why – which was tricky, because the kindly cab driver kept asking – but I remember feeling generally overwhelmed, perhaps by affection, perhaps by realisation of the responsibility I now felt to ensure this book did justice to the man behind the dance routine.

At the time of concluding the manuscript, the most recent series of *Strictly* (Series Ten) had seen Pasha and former Girls Aloud star Kimberley Walsh narrowly miss scooping the winners' title in the 2012 series. It was Pasha's second year in the competition, and his fantastically choreographed performances with the supremely talented Kimberley marked him out as 'one to watch'.

We celebrated the book's publication with lunch in Covent Garden piazza. By this stage, I'd been regaling my friends with regular snippets about Pasha and, as anyone who knows him will tell you, it's really difficult to do that without gushing. As a result of my abundant praise (and penchant for imbuing my social anecdotes with the most miniscule of details), pretty much all of my social circle fell in love with him to varying degrees. This is doubly true of the ones who actually met him, whom I have witnessed visibly swooning in his direction (in a way that would be totally embarrassing, were it not for the fact that everyone does it.)

Once I was describing the glorious, sunny day when Pasha

took me for lunch, and how there was a string quartet and opera singer performing on the cobbled stone floor of the open-air restaurant where we enjoyed an extraordinarily good glass of wine (and endless slivers of cheese), to one of my best friends. Pasha had also given me a gift that day, a beautiful pen – because it was a running joke between us that my skanky old biros would always give up and die halfway through our writing sessions. She listened agog (I swear she started drooling slightly at one point) and was silent in contemplation for a moment, before declaiming, 'OH MY GOD, MAKE HIM MARRY YOU!'

It will come as an immense relief both to my partner and to Pasha's that I don't have any romantic designs on him, but he is the sort of old-fashioned gent who makes you feel wistfully romantic in his company (or even, it would seem, when enjoying it vicariously). On a couple of occasions during the writing process, I became aware that I was gazing at him in a black-and-white-film type of way – something about the combination of his bone structure and the way he draws you in by speaking slowly and deliberately has that effect. The phenomenon is universally effective – even my boyfriend is slightly infatuated with Pasha.

In the next series of *Strictly*, which began in autumn 2013, Pasha was paired with quiz show *Countdown*'s resident brains (and beauty) Rachel Riley. Unlike Kimberley, Rachel's career to date had not afforded her the opportunity to learn the basics of dance, and she made no secret of how she found the routines challenging. Pasha told me he'd incorporated maths, Rachel's natural forte, into the way he taught her the steps, drawing diagrams to make the routines seem more 'logical'. This stroke of tactical genius meant that Rachel made an extraordinary amount of progress in a small amount of time.

Despite this, they left the competition in Week Six, the judges declaring that they could see a lot of potential in Rachel but that her fellow celebrities were learning their craft at a faster pace (something furiously debated and denied on social media afterwards, with many fans believing Rachel had been given a raw deal). There was, in my opinion, something incredibly captivating about watching Pasha and Rachel dance together. While perhaps not the most technically proficient duo (according to the judges, anyway), they had something which cannot be taught – chemistry.

Sometime after the 2013 series was concluded, with Abbey Clancy and her partner Aljaz declared that season's winners, Rachel and Pasha became an item. Pasha is notoriously private about his romantic life – which is unsurprising, given his gentlemanly persona and the maniacal press frenzy which accompanies each series of *Strictly*. It would therefore be incredibly disloyal of me to reveal or speculate upon Pasha and Rachel as a (still relatively new) couple any more than this – I've spent time with them and, as far as I can see, it really works. I'm incredibly fond of Rachel, and I approve of her in the role of Pasha's girlfriend in the way that a friend should. And that really is all I have to say about it.

In 2013, Pasha's former long-term dance partner, Anya Garnis, joined the cast of *Strictly* and was paired with actor Patrick Robinson. The following year, Anya was invited back to dance as part of the ensemble cast but did not have her own celebrity partner. Pasha and Anya had met originally as teenagers in Siberia, dated, moved to America together in their early twenties and, following some reticence on Pasha's part, auditioned together for *So You Think You Can Dance*. It marked the beginning of their respective careers in television, with both of them going on to perform in the show as well as on *Dancing with the Stars*, the American version of *Strictly Come Dancing*.

Pasha and Anya often danced together for the group routines performed every week during *Strictly*'s opening sequences. This was, unsurprisingly, the focal point of a great deal of intrigue from those who read our book. During my research and following its publication, I'd connected with a close-knit and incredibly loyal cabal of hard core (but lovely) Pasha fans online. I even met a couple of them while attending the opening of his 2014 tour with Katya in the West End. (Susie, their ring leader, recognised me and made a beeline straight away, allowing me brief delusions of fame and importance.) To my tremendous relief, Pasha's fans were unanimous in their praise of the book, declaring it had succeeded in capturing the man they adored.

When the first episode of *Strictly* 2013 was broadcast and it was known that Anya had joined the cast, my Twitter timeline was suddenly full of questions – how did Pasha feel about being reunited with her? Didn't they part on frosty terms when he moved to Britain without her? WHAT IS THE GOSSIP?

It will come as no surprise to anyone who was paying attention when I talked about Pasha's disdain for drama and lack of self-importance that I don't know the definitive answer to these questions. I can only say that he seemed characteristically casual about the entire thing.

Here is what I do know: there is no substitute for a shared

history when it comes to dancing. In 2015, Pasha launched a tour called *Life Through Dance*. Although it was in essence a solo tour, in that it contained solely his own concepts and choreography, Pasha invited Anya (plus a cast of four other professional dancers) to perform the show's routines. Seeing Anya and Pasha dance together was a revelation. There is something instinctual in the way they move, which makes sense given how they learned their craft together as part of the same dance school, all those years ago.

Sometimes you forget that Pasha and Anya are dancing a predetermined sequence of steps. Everything is so fluid and their movements are so attuned to one another's, it's as though they are one mind operating two bodies – and the mind is improvising as it goes along. When Anya and Pasha performed his Paso Doble it was so utterly fantastic, so brilliantly executed, that I briefly forgot my own name. One can also forget – when one is in possession of a slightly flabby, distinctly uncoordinated writer's body – how other people's bodies – or at least those that have been practising their artistic discipline virtually since birth – can do extraordinary things that make the human form look so wonderful.

Watching others dance, compared with Pasha and Anya, can only be likened to the difference between someone singing pleasantly enough in tune and someone else conveying emotion from the depths of their soul, in a way that transcends even the need to sing. Except that, if Pasha and Anya were singers, they would be in tune as well, which basically makes them the Aretha Franklins of dancing.

The concept behind *Life Through Dance* is exactly what the title suggests, and it's quintessential Pasha. Each of the routines represents a different fundamental human emotion: attraction, happiness, jealousy – they're all in there and all performances are relatable to anyone in possession of a heart.

Pasha is a connoisseur of human behaviour. It's something that truly great dancers and writers have in common – a need to people-watch in order to enhance their skills. I am, of course, completely and totally biased, but every time I watch *Strictly* I'm struck by Pasha's superior ability to convey a story through his choreography. So when he announced his own tour and said that the theme was going to be how human beings relate to one another, nothing could have made more sense to me.

In his letter to the audience, printed on the opening page of the programme for *Life Through Dance*, Pasha describes dance as 'an international language... which anyone can understand, without the need for translators or dictionaries'. As someone who began his life in Russia, went on to become an American citizen and now resides in Britain, but regularly travels the globe, we can assume that dance is the one constant in Pasha's life, the one way of expressing himself that will be comprehended no matter where he is.

Indeed, it is when he is dancing that Pasha casts off his characteristic *laissez faire*-ness. I have seen him express the full spectrum of human emotion on stage, rendering even ugly feelings like jealousy beautiful through movement. Pasha doesn't just convey feeling through dance, he embodies the emotion – it runs through him, like a bolt of electricity. It is this skill for channelling a vast gamut of moods on stage which is, I believe, what allows him to take things so much in his stride all the rest of the time. After all, if you've experienced wrath, envy, lust and elation already that day in rehearsals, you're hardly likely to lose your shit over a parking ticket.

That's my theory, anyway – and its logical conclusion is that anger management therapy should include ballroom dancing classes, which is something I shall be suggesting to our government's Secretary for Health...

Anyway, I digress. At the time of writing, Pasha and his celebrity dance partner, TV presenter Caroline Flack, are the reigning *Strictly* champions. I've been lucky enough to bump into Caroline on a couple of occasions, and am always struck by how such a tiny person (I could practically fit her in my pocket) can have such an enormous presence and personality. She's witty, with a raucous laugh and a mischievous glint in her eye, and we bonded over the mutual feeling that we were in a platonic relationship with Pasha while we were working with him.

'He's like a brother!' I shouted tipsily in Caroline's direction after one too many cocktails at the 2014 *Cosmopolitan* Woman of the Year Awards. 'Yes! Or a husband… but without the sex!' agreed Caroline, who was significantly more sober than me but apparently has fewer linguistic inhibitions.

Pasha once described to me the ideal trajectory for winning a dance competition like *Strictly* – you start strong, but not at the top of the leaderboard, because then you will have peaked too soon. Somewhere towards the middle of the competition you mark yourself out as a contender for the title. And then, in the last few weeks, you whip out the big guns – the routines that will get you the coveted four tens from the judges. It just so happens that this is the exact course that Pasha and Caroline took in the competition. They received the highest marks ever given during a *Strictly* final. (In fact, Pasha holds the record for the most tens given to any of the professional dancers, which should really make you reassess all the comments I've made heretofore about being biased!)

I was hopping about nervously from one foot to the other, clad in cow-print pyjamas, eyes glued to my television, stress-eating Haribo Starmix, when the final *Strictly* result was announced on 20 December 2014. When Pasha and Caroline's triumph became clear, I immediately texted him to tell him he was brilliant and amazing and deserved it entirely. I received a completely predictable response – modestly acknowledging Caroline's hard work and looking forward to his forthcoming tour. But I wasn't fooled – Pasha's smile as he lifted the legendary Glitterball trophy looked like it was going to break free from his face and take on a life of its own.

The day after his victory, I was asked to write an enlightening few hundred words about Pasha – still seen as something of a charismatic enigma by the British press – for the *Daily Telegraph*. I chose to focus on his approach towards masculinity. I've long been disdainful of the current trend for men defining themselves by pumping iron in the gym, refusing to open doors for women because 'feminism killed chivalry' (it didn't, it just kicked it in the balls), and generally being all style and no substance. It was only when I worked with Pasha that I gained some perspective on what was actually concerning me: how gentlemen, those people who truly understand what being a strong man is, are becoming rarer and rarer. Pasha seemed to encapsulate everything missing from the modern definition of what it means to be a man.

After the piece was published, Rachel Riley tweeted a link to it with the words, 'For Pasha fans (I know there are lots out there!) Here's my favourite in the words of Natasha Devon.'

This stamp of approval signalled to me that I'd got it right. And so I'll leave you with a few words from that article to bear in mind as Pasha takes you on the extraordinary journey that is his life:

Pasha is paradoxical in many ways. He decided he wanted to be a dancer aged seven, because he saw a ballroom show at his local arts centre and saw that there were lots of pretty girls in skimpy costumes. Despite this, I've never known him be remotely disrespectful or sleazy. He's pursued his ambition to dance professionally with steely determination, yet his central philosophy is a dedication to flexibility in the face of obstacles and a laid-back, instinct-led approach to decision making. He's really Russian, really American and a little bit British all at the same time. He's a compassionate soul yet completely allergic to being told what to do.

In short, he isn't afraid to be himself.

Natasha Devon
2015

INTRODUCTION

The first thing I should probably confess is, contrary to what you've heard, my name is not actually Pasha.

In Russia, where I was born and grew up, everyone has a couple of names. There's your 'real' name, the one that's used on all your formal documents (and sometimes when you're in trouble), but you're never really called that by anyone you know. And then there's your 'nickname' – in my case, Pasha.

My 'real' name is Pavel. I'm not sure what the logic behind the abbreviation of my name is or how I came to be named Pasha, especially as it's not actually shorter, but at least they both begin with the same letter. My brother, who is eight years my junior, is technically named Alexandr but everyone calls him Sasha, which doesn't seem to make any sense at all.

I guess the English-speaking world is not exempt from this sort of thing. Peggy is short for Margaret in English, and I've never met anyone who has any idea why. According to Wikipedia, there are standard practices for replacing one letter with another in the world of nicknames, so if you're an etymologist you can probably explain it better than I can. All I know is that, in Russia, it was simply an accepted custom. Everyone does it.

So, today I am called Pasha, but it might interest you to learn that I was very nearly named one of a random selection of twenty other names, some traditional and some just popular in Russia at the time.

Legend has it (or rather the story my mother likes to tell) that, when I was born, my parents didn't know what to call me. I was their firstborn so I suppose they didn't have much experience in baby naming. My mum, Galina, said that she spent the first five days of my life referring to me as 'her boy'. Obviously, this couldn't go on forever, so after Mum came home from the hospital my parents found themselves at a family summit, the purpose of which was to address the very important issue of what was to become my name. My grandma, mother, father and Aunt Marina (who was just 14 at the time) were present, all with a few ideas about what this new addition to the family, their little Siberian baby boy, should be called.

My grandma, Lidia, favoured Kiril or Anton. Her father had been named Kiril and her own middle name was the feminine version of that – Kirilovna. It's another Russian custom to take your father's name as your middle one, and luckily nearly all the traditional names have male and female versions, usually ending in 'vich' for a man and 'na' for a woman.

My mother liked Artem or Maxim. These names were popular

at the time; they were trendy and modern. And my father, Sergei, liked Victor or Alexandr, which eventually became my brother's name, because he had a good friend who was called that.

There was no more sentimental meaning attached to their choice of names than that. Russia was still under Communist rule right up until 1991, so they were not culturally influenced by anything spiritual or religious. Superstition didn't feature in their thinking.

All the names they'd thought of were written down and placed in my dad's traditional Russian rabbit-skin hat, which in Russia we call a *shapka-ushanka* (it literally translates as 'a hat with ears'). In addition to their favourites, they also threw in a few random names. Pavel was one of them. After that, it was left to the hands of fate – or, rather, the small hands of my teenage aunt, who was tasked with selecting one of the names. My mum recently admitted that at first she had a few negative feelings about what was eventually decided. Apparently, when she was growing up, there was a little boy of about the same age who lived in the adjoining apartment block and had the name Pavel. He was, she said, a 'Goodie two-shoes', a musician who was 'always clean' and never wanted to play. His mother used to stand outside the apartment block calling his name when she wanted him to come home. It was that memory that my name first evoked.

But they had agreed that whatever name my aunt would pull out of the hat, this was what my name should be. There was no arguing with it. My name was picked by a young girl's hand and my mother can't even remember now which member of my family actually wrote that name down.

That story of how I came to have my name is significant to me because it seems like it was a blueprint for what was to come. When I look at my life, I can't see that I've had any more power over any of the things that have happened than I did over what I was called. People often talk of 'fate' but, as I understand it, the concept doesn't quite fit with what I believe. 'Fate' suggests you are destined for just one thing and that it's something you can plan for. I believe that, as we navigate life, there are lots of options and the best we can do is be open to those opportunities and not be too rigid in our thinking.

People are often surprised by how laid-back I am by nature. I suppose it's because Russians have a reputation for being a little aggressive and dancers for being fiery and passionate. I thwart people's expectations by having a mild temperament and a relaxed attitude.

When people ask me how I became a success in an industry where so many try and fail to 'make it', I simply say I was open to the possibility. I'm relaxed, I'm open and the opportunities present themselves for me to grab. Every decision I have made has been decided by my gut, not my head. I've done what felt right at the time, and I haven't regretted a single moment.

When you anticipate the future, or plan things down to the finest detail, you miss all the other wonderful, random possibilities life throws at you. People get so caught up in trying to control every aspect of their lives, they get bogged down in the detail and they don't see that there were always other names in the hat.

Chapter 1

THE LITTLE DANCING BEAR

I began my career performing in stage shows, living and working in studios and art centres throughout Russia, before moving to the US.

I have only ever wanted to dance. I'm happy to do it on stage or as a teacher and my foray into television happened entirely by accident, as you'll discover later. However it came about, I'm probably best known for taking part in two hugely popular television shows: *So You Think You Can Dance* over in the US and *Strictly Come Dancing* in the UK, where I now live.

The great thing about working on these TV shows is that everything is planned out for us. All I have to think about, during the periods when I'm rehearsing and filming *Strictly*, is my next dance. All the little worries in life, the things that usually occupy my mind on a day-to-day basis, are taken away and my existence becomes 100 per cent about the show and the dancing.

I like the feeling of being totally absorbed by dance. It reminds me of the very first moment when I decided to become a dancer. I was seven years old and visiting the arts and sports centre where my grandmother worked, back in Siberia.

My Russian hometown was called Komsomolsk-na-Amure. It was established in 1932 after it was built from nothing. Developers literally fabricated an entire town from the air that existed before it, out in the sparse Siberian countryside. They then made a nationwide call for Russians who wanted to move there and start a new life.

The town was nicknamed the *gorod Yu nosti*, which in English translates to the 'city of youth'. This was because the town itself was so young and because of all the opportunity, energy and prosperity the name conjures up. To move there was seen as exciting; everything was completely new.

Designed by architects from St Petersburg, the town had wide, open avenues interspersed with parks and trees. Everything about it was designed for purpose and made-to-measure. It was actually quite beautiful in its functionality yet with none of the quirky charm that I now know there is in other towns and cities throughout the world. Everything had a grey pallor and every street looked the same.

As a young boy, I used to escape to the little parks and wooded areas in our town, where I would try to transform my little grey world using only my imagination and nature as tools. I'd find branches and twigs, which I'd pretend were swords, or I'd fashion something that was like a rudimentary bow and arrow. I would create a character for myself – he was an adventurer and a huntsman – and then I'd go to explore and hunt my prey.

For me, those woodlands became magical enchanted forests, places where I could escape the mundane and explore the recesses of my mind. I was fascinated by nature. It seemed to me like a whole new world, laid out for me to discover.

Outside the parks, there wasn't much for a curious, creative young boy like me to play with. Everything was minimal and painted in the same dull palette. The town was filled with large, square factories, which produced atomic submarines and fighter jets. My mother worked in one of those factories and my dad drove a truck that collected and delivered construction materials like stone and sand. I definitely didn't come from a dancing dynasty! My parents' professions were far from where my path would eventually lead me.

My mum later told me she used to dream of being a beautiful ballerina. She didn't mean that was her true ambition in life, in the way that Americans and Brits use the word 'dream', she literally meant that she would dream about it as she slept. Dance was clearly important to her in some way. I think in retrospect that was part of the reason she was so supportive when I left home at a relatively early age to study dance at boarding school.

In 1980 when I was born, right up until when I was 11 years old, Russia was under Communist rule. Society didn't work in the way that people are used to in the US and the UK. Everything was free, from your housing, schooling and health to your recreation.

There was a pride associated with working hard to contribute to the smooth running of our Russian society. Everyone worked so that everyone could live. Conversation always centred on what was 'real': we didn't read horoscopes, people didn't practise religion; work was central to our psyche and day-to-day existence. The reality was that you had to work, and working was the basis of your reality.

There were a couple of huge sports and arts centres in my town, and these were replicated throughout Russia. We could go there to take part in lots of sports and leisure activities and they were mainly to give the kids something to do. Again, the government provided these for us, free of charge.

One day in February 1987, my mum took me to our local arts centre to see a ballroom dance show. Of course, winter in Siberia is very cold (although one of the greatest myths is that Siberia is *always* cold. They do have brief warm summers there, contrary to what people believe). Wrapped up in layer upon layer of fur to protect me from the elements, I wore a fur coat and hat, as well as mittens on an elastic band. I looked and felt like a little Russian bear, bundled in so much furry get-up.

As we watched local young people dance ballroom and Latin, the explosion of colour and movement enchanted me. I had never seen anything like it before. The vivid pinks, yellows and greens contrasted so sharply with the bleak urban townscape that was then my world.

There were a dozen or so female ballroom dancers spinning, shimmying and twirling so that they almost melted into one vibrant rainbow. Of course, they must have had male partners too, but I don't remember seeing them at all. I now know that the boys must have been dressed in black and white and that is probably why they didn't leave any impression on me.

I can't pretend there wasn't a part of me that didn't fall in love with those girls in their skimpy little costumes either. They seemed to me, even at such a young age, irresistibly sexy. I always find it funny that one of the most frequent Google

4

searches associated with my name is people questioning whether I might be gay when one of the first things that attracted me to my craft was the opportunity to work with beautiful, semi-naked girls! But I suppose that sort of speculation happens with every male dancer, especially one as private about his relationship with his girlfriend as I am.

So this little Russian bear sat completely mesmerised by what he saw. And it was then that I decided whatever it was they were doing, whatever enchantment they were creating, I wanted to be a part of it. Since then, dancing has never lost its magical quality for me. To dance has always been to enter into another reality, whether it's on stage, in the studio or on television; dance feels like the ultimate expression. Even now I am struggling to put into words what I could so much more easily show you through movement.

Right from the very first second I saw ballroom dancing in action it captured me and nothing else mattered. After that day, it seemed I was constantly in lessons, which took place three times per week, or training or practising, in the small purpose-built studios at the sports centre, and eventually I left home, aged 14, to join my dance group in a different city. People often ask me if I feel as though I missed out on the 'normal' things children do because, from that moment on, my whole life was completely dedicated to dance. I don't think like that. Happily, my circumstances dictate that I was able to do what I wanted, and I'm grateful to be able to continue to do dance to this day.

I must have been one determined little bear because, as soon as she could, my mum signed me up for freestyle dance, jazz and ballet lessons. I was the only boy in my class.

I can't say I minded.

As a young boy, I loved to read. I began reading when I was about five years old and I've loved books ever since, although I've had less and less time to devote to reading as I've grown older. I remember taking a book with me to school when I was very young and sitting reading it instead of listening to my teacher. I would finish on average a book in a day, taking a different one in each time. In this regard I take after my father, who, I seem to recall, was always reading when he was at home, selecting a book from the shelves and shelves of them we had in our apartment.

The September after that first day in February when I fell in love with ballroom, I began dance classes at a studio on the other side of town. During the time in between, I'd been doing a little jazz, freestyle and ballet at my grandma's arts centre in preparation. The arts centre was attached to a park, right in the centre of town. It was the biggest place for arts and sport in town and a favourite place for the locals to go. My grandma used to work in the café and she would sneak me pastries whenever I would go there. Perhaps that is where my love of sweets originated. It seemed like a magic place for me to go. I used to imagine it was a castle. I loved exploring it and would look forward to going there to visit my grandma. The thing I remember most about those classes in the spring and summer was getting into trouble with my teacher, who was very strict and didn't like the way I talked to – and distracted – the female students!

Getting to my ballroom classes in the new academic year involved a lot of walking and a bus journey across town. As I sat, usually shivering, on the bus, I'd read Russian fables. Even though the ancient, trundling old vehicle was freezing-cold

6

(unless you managed to get the seat next to the heater, which was rare), I actually looked forward to the opportunity of 40 minutes or so to read, uninterrupted.

I began by reading traditional Russian folk stories. There was one, I remember, about an old farmer and his wife who had a chicken that laid a golden egg. They were so happy with the egg, until one day some mice ran by, causing the egg to fall to the ground and break. The old couple began crying but the chicken comforted them and promised to lay them another golden egg, which made them happy again. As far as I can remember, that was the whole story. I'm not sure what the moral was supposed to be – I think it made more sense in Russian!

As I grew older, I began to get into science fiction stories, more than the fables I used to read as an infant. Science fiction was one of the main ways we had access to foreign writers in Russia at that time. But there was one story I'd come back to again and again. It was a tale of a very manly, strong American cowboy who was exploring the Wild West. I loved that book, perhaps because I used to fantasize about being an explorer when I played in the woodlands of my hometown; I really identified with that cowboy. I started to think of the US as an exciting place. My love of American culture definitely began a long time before I actually moved there, in my twenties.

All of my favourite stories to read involved a journey, even if it was a trip to Mars or Venus. During this period of my childhood, if I wasn't dancing then I was reading, exploring or reading about exploring! The more I learned about dance, the more the other activities started to whittle away, though.

Dancing began to dominate my life. It wasn't a bad thing – I just lost interest in doing anything else.

I remember the first time I danced in public. It was around six months after I started dance classes and I was eight years old. It was part of a group number and we had to have costumes. We didn't have much money at the time so my mum had to make me something to wear from scratch.

When I look back, no one ever seemed to have much money in my town at the time. Communism was falling apart and Russia was moving towards democracy. Even the simplest things stopped being readily available and rationing was commonplace. We were given tickets for items such as sugar and meat, and sometimes the queues for this produce would last for hours, even days. Seeing this made me realise that something must be happening politically in Russia, and that the huge empire of the USSR must be falling apart. Until then, Moscow, where I knew all the politics happened, seemed so far away that it just wasn't relevant to us in Siberia.

There wasn't much variety in what we ate because supplies were so scarce and clothing tended to be very basic. So, for my costume, Mum made me a tunic from thick, shiny material and every night she sat sewing on thousands of silver sequins, one by one, until the entire front was covered. It must have taken her two weeks to complete it and, when it was finished, it was the most astonishing garment I had ever seen up to that point. I remember feeling so proud, dancing and sparkling during my performance.

The desire to dance was so strong that when my coach told me he was moving to another studio further away, and he wanted me and some other students to follow him, it seemed obvious that I would go. We all became attached to our coaches and at the time it was unthinkable for me that I would ever work with anyone else.

My teacher was called Sergey Pushkov, but we never used to refer to him by his last name. We would address him using his first and middle names, which were Sergey Pavlovich. That was the formal way to address anyone in authority like a teacher, or in a work environment, in Russia. He was part of a team of coaches at the studio who worked together. Each coach's students would compete against each other in organised dance contests within the studio. This instilled a sense of competition in us from very early on. I only ever saw Sergey dance properly, with a partner, once. He had a very pretty girlfriend, who was also his dance partner. She came to the studio one day for a local competition, wearing a beautiful, long orange dress, and they danced a waltz. After that, she moved away and we never saw her again.

Sergey seemed really old to me at the time, although I suppose looking back he must have been only about 20 years old. He wasn't a tall man and he had a skinny frame, so, overall, he was fairly diminutive. There were five students who were asked to go with Sergey to a different studio in the same town; we were all about nine or 10 years old at the time. The older, more experienced teenagers in the studio used to lend a hand in training us younger kids.

But it didn't seem odd to me to be moving to a studio further away because that was simply the ways things were done. It was the accepted order that you moved with your teacher if you were asked and that you were part of a dancing community. The five of us joined a class of about 20 in total. In the end, only

9

three of us stayed. There was another boy called Pasha and my dance partner, Oksana.

Oksana was really gorgeous. She had dark, glossy hair, olive skin and her eyes were almost black. She was also a really talented dancer. Her mother was a very prominent figure, I remember, and quite forceful. She made sure that she had her say on everything our studio did, from the competitions we entered to the dances we performed and the costumes we wore. Oksana's father had left the family home and wasn't around any longer, so her mother raised her alone. Her mum managed to make better money on her own than both of my parents' incomes combined. She'd also brought Oksana up to be very proper and to have impeccable manners.

In our new studio, there was one boy who everyone talked about as being super-talented. His best dances were the Latin ones, especially the rumba and cha-cha-cha. His movements were extremely fluid, flexible and languid. Back then, I didn't think of myself as being a very good dancer. I remember feeling that my movements were rigid compared to his. I felt like Pinocchio, the little wooden boy from the story, when dancing next to him. I wasn't exactly jealous, but I do recall how I would compare myself to him.

The director and main coach at my studio, Irina Gabdrakhmanova (we called her Irina Yurievna), used to be constantly telling me I wasn't that good at dancing as well. Later, I found out that her background wasn't actually anything to do with ballroom dancing: she had been an aerobics teacher at the leisure centre where she had previously worked. She then discovered that she had a talent for putting together shows and organising her students into formations, so she was asked to coach the dancers at her new place. Looking back, when she would tell me I couldn't dance, I have no idea what that criticism was based on. I would always try to respond with something that made my point, but I was cut short and told to be quiet.

None of this made me despondent, however, and I certainly never thought about giving up. It's just within my character to be quite independent from the opinions of others. I still don't let negative feedback have any effect on me other than to make me work harder. So that's exactly what I did.

I remember the turning point came the first time I won a competition, when I was 11 years old. It was a regional event, where students from various dance studios came together. I danced three dances: a mixture of Latin and standard ballroom. As I took first place, I realised that my victory must mean I was becoming a better dancer, despite what Irina had said. What do you know? I can do this, I thought to myself.

That was the day I started reading less and practising my dance more.

Chapter 2

WANT TO BE
IN MY GANG?

When people think of artistic or media-based environ-
ments, like dance, for some reason they always think of
them as being defined by cliques and one-upmanship.
Certainly, movies present it that way: one person gets to be the
'star' and everyone else wants to be them. This always leads to
tension and the creation of a 'hero' and a 'villain'.

I've never been particularly affected by cliques, or been
motivated by wanting to be popular. When people around me
squabble or there are unspoken tensions that others perceive,
it just seems to go over my head. Maybe I'm simply not
attuned to these things. Even now, when people ask me to
comment on the gossip that always appears in the newspapers
about my fellow *Strictly Come Dancing* professionals, I have to
tell them that I wouldn't know. I just don't pay attention to
anything like that.

When I look back on my childhood, I don't remember being envious of friends or 'breaking up' with anyone in my dance studio. We were definitely taught to have a fierce sense of rivalry whenever we competed against one another in dance contests but we never carried that sense of competition back to the studio, or took it out on each other privately. That's not to say I wasn't aware of my family's financial situation when I was growing up or how that made me compare to the other kids I danced with. I was mindful of their having more material things than I did. We never had much money, although I cannot say I was ever especially bothered by it, and my mum made sure we had everything we needed. Even though we relied on rationing when I lived at home, I never recall feeling hungry; we just didn't have the luxuries.

I remember there was one kid in particular in our class who always had the best costumes for shows, and it seemed like every week he had a new pair of shoes. He was the first person I ever knew to own a computer. It was a little handset, in the style of a very early Game Boy, with a slot where you could put tapes in the back to load the game. I would sometimes go to his house to have a play on it. It was lots of fun and a novelty for me after being used to playing in the woods with sticks and using my imagination. That was when my love affair with computer games began. It's something I still like to do.

When I went to boarding school, whose name was 'Middle Boarding School Number One' (all the schools were numbered in Russia at the time, rather than given names) my favourite teacher actually had a couple of computers in his classroom. My physics teacher was a tall, imposing man, who looked very serious and always seemed to have a textbook in his hand. He was fascinated by computers, which were still quite rare in Russia at that stage. In other parts of the world, like America, PCs were commonplace and they had advanced as far as getting the first portable phones, but in Russia we existed really without any kind of technology. Believe it or not, I didn't get my first computer until 2001 when I was living in the States and was living in New York. Up until then, I hadn't thought I needed one.

I was 10 years old when I went away to boarding school. My new dance studio was an hour's journey away from home so it was better for me to have somewhere to live nearby if rehearsals ran until late at night (which they invariably did, we usually finished around 9 or 10pm).

People ask me how I felt about going to live at school, so young. I can only repeat what I said before, that it didn't feel like a choice and I didn't think about it for long. There was always a sense of what I'd call a 'studio spirit', as if we belonged to a little pack. We dancers had a huge sense of loyalty and that's why we would follow our studio coaches from place to place, preferring to stay with them.

When Irina moved to the town, she brought with her some of the students from the studio she had been working in before. They were also boarders at the school, like me. I would go home at weekends. The rest of my friends from the studio attended as day schoolers because they lived closer to the studio than I did. There were older members of my studio there at the school too, but they were well into their teens and kept their distance. They didn't tend to communicate with us younger students that much outside of dance class. Although they didn't shun us exactly, they were just too cool to be seen hanging around with 10-year-olds.

There were only 120 students in the entire school, although the building itself was absolutely huge, at least it seemed that way to me at the time. It had two wings: one for girls and one for boys. It was a school for orphans and for dancers; there were also some kids there with non-contagious tuberculosis. We dancers didn't tend to mix much with the others. This wasn't for any other reason than our timetables were different; we were exempt from the usual rules and school schedule.

Dance rehearsals took priority over everything else, including our studies. We got to train every single day and our academic teachers respected that and built classes around our dancing. There was an unspoken understanding that we were there to dance before we were there to learn the subjects more traditionally taught in school.

I remember boarding school being a really happy time. Mainly I spent my days with other dancers my own age from the studio. We had a lot of freedom and were often left to our own devices. We'd spend the whole day together and felt like we were undertaking a voyage together, as part of our little clan. There were no 'best friends' and no enemies; it simply felt like an exciting adventure.

I only have what I would describe as bright memories from that place. Even though it was cold and the walls of the building were what you would technically describe as grey, it always seemed colourful to me.

My fondest memories are of the times when dance practice would mean we would miss the communal supper with the other students. This used to happen quite a lot because our dance schedule was really hectic, even then. When we came back into the main building after training, the cooks would have left us huge pots of whatever it was they had prepared that day for the other students. About 10 of us from the studio would sit for hours, feasting and talking, while the rest of the school was sleeping.

Even though I was a cheeky student whose knowledge of books made him think he knew everything, perhaps, looking back, I was given too much freedom at boarding school, although I struggle to think of a happier and less complicated time. Those midnight feasts, in particular, taught me what I loved in life – food, friends and feeling special because I was a dancer.

Chapter 3

GROWING UP

I was 14 years old when the time came for me to move on again. Our coach, Irina, had been invited to another town. This town, which was called Kemerovo, was still within Siberia but the area is so vast that it was actually 2,000 miles away from where we were before.

This time, because of the distance involved, not everyone at my studio found it such an easy decision to move on as a pack and stay together. Again, the older students who had come with Irina in the first place moved with her, and, again, there were six of us within my age category who were given the opportunity to go to the new studio. The 'super-talented' boy who used to dance the competent, languid Latin dances I'd so admired was of course one of the original six, but in the end he was just too attached to his family and his hometown to make the decision to leave with us.

In the end, there were four of us who were prepared to up sticks and trek across the country with Irina. My dance partner, Oksana, was one of them, although she stayed less than a year, as it turned out. I think this was the time when it really hit us that, if we were serious about putting dancing above all else, it would take a lot of personal sacrifice. Other people struggled with it more than I did. For me, it just seemed like the natural thing to do.

I'd become very independent. By that point, I was aware of my own independence and I found it exciting. I thought of myself as a man because I'd been so used to making my own rules and having very little supervision or routine. I don't remember my mum getting involved or having her say in the decision for me to move again, although she was supportive when I told her. It was easy for me to say yes because I'd become attached to the lifestyle of being a dancer. Being torn away from the familiarity of the people I'd been dancing with for six years would have been so much more difficult to deal with; moving to new territory seemed trivial by comparison.

My new home was in the centre of Siberia. The climate there was a lot rougher than I had been used to. Even now I shiver when I remember how cold it was and how vicious the winds were. It was a coal-mining town and a regional capital, so it was big compared to the places I'd lived before. In a way, it seemed simpler than my hometown because it was so sparse – everything was spread out. It was still predominantly painted in various shades of grey, but the buildings were far grander and the place had better shopping facilities and nightlife than I had known before. It was while I lived here that I had my first ever experience of going to a restaurant. Here, eating out was commonplace and they had a restaurant on every corner, but at home, if we had any, I didn't notice. No one I knew from back home ever used to eat out, or mention eating out. It wasn't part of the culture of my hometown.

The Governor of the region had invited our dance studio to the town to fulfil the criteria of their arts programme. A Governor was in charge of each Russian constituency, it is the highest office a person can hold other than President. By then, our studio had gained a reputation for putting on great shows all over Russia. The older dancers had travelled much further than we had, up to that point. I had mostly competed in regional competitions but the dancing of our studio had been noticed and admired much further afield.

There was a shortage of apartments in our new hometown so we were put into temporary accommodation as part of the deal the Governor made for us moving there. We were in a square block of little rooms also being used as temporary accommodation for those who worked in a nearby coal mine.

After Oksana left, there were only two dancers of my age from the original studio – me and another boy, Dan, with whom I shared a room. Dan danced with Irina's daughter, Lena, which meant that he was in a good position and always being selected for contests. Again, this wasn't something that worried or particularly irked me; it was simply something I observed. He and I were actually great friends and there were four or five years of our lives when we were like peas in a pod. Not only did we stay in the same room, but we also ate from the same plate. You'd rarely see one of us without the other in tow.

I had to start work at 14. The government had paid for the first two years of my dance lessons, which were undertaken in groups, and this was standard under their education programme. As I got better and began competing, I had to take private lessons with my dance partner. My parents paid a nominal fee for these. It was unheard of for anything to be paid for in full; because of how Communism works, people expected most things to be free or to pay only a little towards them. When I moved away, though, I knew that, to be truly independent, I had to start supporting myself.

I began teaching dance to younger children as a way of making ends meet. There was a lot of work around for me to do, and soon I was making more money than my mum did. That didn't stop her from sending me a little cash every now and then, though. I didn't need it, but it was her way of showing care during a time when I was only seeing my family once a year during the summer for a week or two. The money represented my mum's support and love so I always accepted it.

Even though I was making good money for my age, I still had to be frugal in order to survive. Quite often dinner would be just a loaf of bread and a can of condensed milk (which is actually delicious, in addition to being cheap). If I had enough money to treat myself, I'd cook dumplings with a bag of shrimp or I'd buy a bar of chocolate.

Chocolate has always been special to me. I have a very sweet tooth and chocolate wasn't a common foodstuff in Siberia in the 1980s as it is today. It was a rare treat, which made it all the more delicious. There were cheaper, hard candies that people would suck on, but they didn't have the same appeal. I remember once my dad brought home a huge bag of broken chocolate pieces. He was doing a job transporting chocolate and this was a bag of what I suppose you'd call remnants, that weren't suitable for sale. Some of the lumps of chocolate in that bag were bigger than my head! I cannot even tell you how happy it made me.

I also remember once watching a Polish kid's fairytale movie about a prince and princess. In one scene, the prince brought the princess chocolate with nuts in it. To me, it was a revelation that chocolate could contain nuts. I remember thinking what a treat that would be and actually falling in love with the idea of nutty chocolate. Even now, if I have some change in my pocket, I'm most likely to spend it on chocolate.

In today's culture, it would be unusual for someone as young as 16 to be working and living so far away from home, but I never felt like I missed out on anything. I never felt alone, abandoned or deprived of anything. It seemed to me that other kids my age spent a lot of their time feeling fed up because they were doing absolutely nothing; I was always doing something. During the hours I had off, I would be content just to read. I'm very comfortable in my own company. In the whole of my life, I can never recall feeling bored.

Dancing was what I wanted to do and I always got to do what I wanted – how many people can say that?

When we would rehearse in the studio, all the new musical tracks that we danced to came from the West. We had traditional Latin and ballroom music but we'd mix that up with more modern stuff, mainly from the States. Of course, we didn't understand what any of the words meant because we didn't understand English, but that didn't stop us from singing along. We heard the songs so often that the actual phonetic sound the words made would be stuck in our heads and we were able to memorise them. We used to pretend that we could speak English because it seemed to us this was an indicator of being cool. In reality, we didn't know what we were singing, so we used to invent meanings.

I remember we would sometimes do our warm-up to MC Hammer's 'Can't Touch This', which I turned into 'kim-chose-tis' when I sang along, because to me that's what it sounded like.

Later in my life, when I moved to the States and learned English, I realised that the meanings we'd given these songs were totally wrong. Often the tone of the music was completely different to the content of the lyrics. I got a whole new perspective on the songs that I thought I already knew.

One particular moment that seemed poignant was when I finally realised what Gwen Stefani was singing about in the song 'Don't Speak'. As a teenager, the only words I understood of that song were 'you and me' and 'together' but none of the words in between. I knew what 'you and me together' meant, and so I assumed it must be a really romantic love song because it's slow and sort of dreamy in tone. I didn't know it was a song about heartbreak and a relationship ending.

During training, we used to warm up to that song and I'd sing it to my then girlfriend, Anya, not knowing I wasn't singing her a love ballad. I remember we sometimes used to mouth the words 'you and me' and 'together' to each other from across the studio. I thought of it as 'our song', which made me laugh once I realised what it was really about.

Anya joined my dance studio when I was 16 and she was a year younger. She came because the older boys needed someone to partner them in their dances and there was a shortage of girls. For some reason, the boys seemed to remain quite consistently with our studio, but the girls were always coming and going.

Being similar in age and in the dance studio together every single day meant that our entire group inevitably became close, but with Anya it was something more than just a friendship. Right from the moment when she arrived at the studio, I was attracted to her, and, by the time I was 18, we were dating. At first, we kept our romance a secret from everyone – we just thought that we should. Looking back, I'm not sure why. Maybe it was simply the fun of sneaking around and having our own little world that no one else was allowed to be a part of.

Half a year later, we were placed together as dance partners. I wasn't keen on the idea of dancing with my girlfriend, especially since me and my dance partner at the time were going to Moscow and winning a lot of national competitions, but we didn't have any say in the matter. It was tough to maintain a personal relationship and to dance with that same person. If the day's training, or a competition hadn't gone well, it was difficult not to let frustrations about the dancing spill over into our private time.

Our coach believed that on the dance floor the girls should be quiet and submissive and the man must always lead. That way, if the step didn't work out or the dance went wrong, you knew the fault was with the male partner. We had always followed that protocol and I would always be making suggestions on our routines, but Anya was very opinionated and didn't always agree with what I said. The conflict created by this nearly always ended with us being really mean to each other and we'd stop talking for the rest of the day. It's funny but I don't remember us ever falling out about anything else. It was always tension from the dance floor we carried with us into our free time, rather than the other way around.

As it turned out, my relationship with Anya was central to many of the decisions I would make over the course of the next years of my life. When she left the studio for Moscow, a year after we began dancing together, it seemed obvious that I would follow and we'd continue to enter competitions as partners. Shortly afterwards, we left Russia together and travelled to the States, remaining part of a couple, both personally and professionally.

When we were in the US, we broke up but continued to dance together and remained great friends. There are lots of things that turned out to be crucial in shaping my path that wouldn't have happened without Anya's influence. When I became ill in New York, for example, she was the one who persuaded me to go to hospital and to get a diagnosis that turned out to save my life. She was also the one who dragged me to the auditions for *So You Think You Can Dance*. Up until that point, I'd never had any aspirations to be on television but she persuaded me that we should go for it, as a double act.

When I got the call from *Strictly Come Dancing* in 2011 to say they wanted me as one of their professional dancers, I did what I always do when weighing up any situation and left it to my gut to decide. It felt right to come to Britain for a while and to take part in the show. Unfortunately, *Strictly* weren't looking for any female professionals at that time, which meant breaking up a dance partnership that had lasted for 12 years up until that point.

Anya found it hard to accept that I was taking a job without her. I think she felt I should have told *Strictly* we come as a double act or not at all. Unfortunately, I'd learned enough from *So You Think You Can Dance* to realise that show business doesn't work like that. There are hundreds of people desperate for an opportunity like the one *Strictly Come Dancing* gave me, and I knew I'd regret not grabbing that chance. I tried to explain how I saw it, but Anya felt betrayed. At first television had been her dream, not mine, and now I was being given a chance that she had coveted. She didn't think it was fair.

Ultimately, Anya couldn't get over her belief that I had done her wrong in breaking up our partnership after a six-year love affair and twice as long as that as a dancing team. I don't have any contact with her now but she was my first serious love and I will never forget how knowing her shaped the course of things to come.

Chapter 4

BOY TO
MAN

The mining town is where I really grew up. I arrived as a kid who could barely afford to buy himself a dinner. By the time I was 18, I was teaching, winning competitions and supporting myself with a lifestyle that a lot of Russian adults much older than me could only dream of achieving.

It cost a lot of money to fund my dancing and none of the income I made was really disposable. I still needed a lot of tuition and a different costume for every competition I danced. Most of my money went towards developing my skill. I learned to live quite a basic lifestyle outside of the dance studio. Even now, I would not say I really 'need' much in order to be comfortable. My landlady in Notting Hill recently told me that she thinks my flat looks as though nobody lives there. Everything I consider essential – my personal computer, my clothes and some vitamins – all fits into one bag. I don't even own a television (if I want to watch something, I watch movies on my laptop, and I can review my live *Strictly* performances on YouTube). There's nothing material I can think of that I am particularly attached to.

I finished school aged 18, during my time in the mining town, and I was studying dance, but I never completed my education because I moved to Moscow. I was never in one place long enough to allow me the time I needed to complete my studies. I always had it in my mind that I'd go back and finish college one day, until I got to America, when it dawned on me that having a skill and some common sense was enough to make a living. I was always in demand for my services as a dancer. Besides, I was educated to a reasonable degree and, perhaps most importantly, I was happy.

One day, while we were still in the mining town, out of the blue, Anya told me she was moving to Moscow. She had been told that she was going to be dancing with the boyfriend of our dance coach, Irina, instead of me and she really didn't want to do this. As I said before, we didn't get any say in who we danced with, so it was either do as she was told or leave the studio; Anya chose to leave.

She asked me to come with her but, at first, I didn't have the guts to follow her. Up until then, being part of the studio and the lifestyle that came with it was all I had ever known. Anya was moving to live with her family in the capital and to follow on my own seemed like a scary prospect. I contemplated going, but it felt as though my life at that stage revolved around the dance studio. The studio also had a great reputation in the region and I felt as if my own identity as a dancer was tied up in the brand.

Up until that stage, I had always lived my life as part of a group. My studio felt like a young family and we were knitted together by our common history and our loyalty to one another. Six months after Anya's departure, however, there seemed to be a shift in the way I was thinking about my future. I started to notice things that seemed unjust to me, and it made the studio seem not such a great place any more. Irina's boyfriend was always given the lead roles in dance contests. He would return home from jobs all over Russia and Europe, and start flashing around a big wodge of American dollars – a highly respected currency in our country at the time – or he'd show us his new, expensive watch. I didn't hate him for showing off, but I didn't think that it was right that he was always given the best opportunities. He was clearly being shown favouritism, while it was my opinion that everything should be fair.

When I used to try to argue my point of view with Irina, she would say, 'You're too smart for your own good, you should read less and shut up,' just as she used to when I first knew her, as a small boy. It frustrated me that she was still talking to me like she did when I was a kid. From the age of 14, I'd had to be very independent, and from about 16 onwards I remember that I felt that I wanted to be taken seriously by her and spoken to like an adult.

Looking back now, all of the disputes that we had within the studio seem so unimportant, but at the time it was enough to make me decide to leave and go solo. There were two other dancers who felt the same way, and we all left together. One of them was the other boy named Pasha, who told me he had never felt like he was part of the team at the studio and he believed that he would get better opportunities if he tried on his own. There was also another guy named Denis.

Something about how I was now making my own wage and gaining increasing independence at that time in my life made me suddenly understand that I didn't owe anything to anyone, and that made it a much easier decision to leave the studio. I was craving another adventure, so it seemed logical to follow Anya to Moscow.

It wasn't just Anya who drew me to Moscow, though. To be considered one of the best dancers in Russia, really you had to be in the capital city. In my industry, Moscow was where it all happened.

I'd been to Moscow before for dance competitions, so the place wasn't completely alien to me. The city had always held a fascination for me, from my earliest visit; it was so huge and grand. It was bigger than anything I'd ever seen before that point – the streets just seemed totally overwhelming, in an exciting way. When I moved to Moscow, I'd never been on a subway before. Riding the underground train system there was like playing with a new toy. It sounds an odd thing to say, but I'd never seen people gathering to all travel in one direction together and I was attracted to the idea.

Russians say that life in Moscow is *Kipit*, which translates as 'boiling'. When you boil water, it bubbles at the surface and, when water bubbles, it usually means it is travelling some-where. Shallow water bubbling over stones moves at a fast pace, whereas deep water is still and tranquil. Moscow is like shallow water, hurrying to the next place, so that's where the description of it as 'boiling' comes from.

There were people and cars everywhere, as well as restaurants and stores I'd never even heard of. The travelling time to get from one side of the city to the other was immense. It seemed like you could never do two things in one day.

I arrived in Moscow with no money and no connections, a suburban young man in a big city, to try to generate a career and a new life out of nothing. Irina's studio had been a kind of makeshift family for so long and now I was embarking on life totally alone.

Chapter 5

FAREWELL, MOSCOW

It took me six months after Anya leaving to pluck up the courage to relocate without the support of a studio behind me.

As I said, when I did show up in Moscow, I had nothing – no money, no connections – I had to try to generate work prospects out of thin air. During this time, I even started looking into alternative jobs in offices and stores just to make a living.

I remember going through a period of uncertainty at that stage. People came to the capital from all over Russia to try to achieve their dreams; Moscow didn't need another new kid from suburbia. That was part of where the sense of it 'boiling' came from, all the energy of these outsiders, so enthusiastic and so hopeful about fulfilling their ambitions. I was just one of thousands of non-natives trying to make it and for the first time in my life, I was struggling.

When things weren't going well, I started looking for answers. I wanted to understand why, having always been provided for, I was suddenly experiencing this dry spell. That's when I began taking an interest in books on psychology and the nature of humanity. I became endlessly fascinated by the things we want, as human beings, and why we want them. Now I had a completely new perspective and that meant that I stopped wanting to read science fiction; my interest was right back here on Planet Earth.

I remember reading many books by the same Russian author, Vladimir Zhikarentchev, which talked about how to navigate life with a positive attitude and reach your goals. They addressed topics such as whether or not there is such a thing as karma, the reasons people have the problems they do, and the ways in which you can change. It was then that I hit on an idea: maybe I didn't have to work for someone. Maybe I could work for myself. Every day I would walk around Moscow, going into kindergarten schools. I told them I'd been teaching dance since I was 14, which was true because of the experience I'd gained at the studio, and offered my services as a tutor. One of the schools offered me a position teaching dance classes to three- and four-year-olds. While there, parents advised me on where dance education was needed in other areas of the city, so I approached those schools too.

I found a little area to teach dance in an ice hockey arena. They wanted to hold some dance classes and needed a teacher. Someone had organised some lessons and then disappeared, leaving behind a lot of people eager to learn dance so they asked me to step in. It was a big room with a hardwood floor, like a basketball court, and I used it as a makeshift studio for my new clients, who were a mixture of children and adults.

While doing that, I met the President of the Sports Association, whose 11-year-old son wanted to learn how to dance. Through that connection I managed to get myself into a second college, which if I had ever finished the course would have made me a proper ballroom dance coach, with the papers to prove it. Little by little, my reputation grew. Two years after I first arrived in Moscow, I realised I had what were actually a few different businesses and, finally, I was starting to make enough money.

As soon as I moved to Moscow, I began living with Anya and it was our first experience of living together, rather than just dating. That was the first time I realised there could be hardships in a romantic relationship. I'd only ever lived with boys before and that had seemed much less complicated; this was uncharted territory. I think if we had continued to live in Moscow then we might have split up after a relatively short amount of time but, before that happened, we were invited to move to America.

Anya and I had a friend from her old studio called Andrei, who was living in the States. He had been in Anya's original dance studio, and then all three of us had danced together in the Siberian mining town. Andrei moved to Moscow before Anya and I did because he, just like us, had been having disagreements with Irina. During one of the fights they'd had, he'd called her 'old lady'. Irina hadn't taken kindly to this and had kicked him out.

While in Moscow, Andrei had been given the opportunity, through his dance partner, Galina, to move to the States. Andrei's partner knew a studio owner over in New York who needed a dancing couple. They both applied for visas but she didn't get hers. This was quite common. At the time, it was really difficult to get the right paperwork to enter the USA; the conditions were very strict. Andrei didn't want to miss the opportunity so he went to New York City without his partner in the end.

In August 2000, we got a call from Andrei letting us know that he'd met a studio owner over there and had been talking to him about Anya and me. The studio was called the Fred Astaire Dance Studio and it was a franchise of one of a hugely popular trademark. There are chains of Fred Astaire Dance Studios all over the USA. They focused mainly on social dancing, he told me. The studio was looking for a couple of professional dancers and Andrei thought of us.

Anya and I talked about the possibility of a move. At the time, she was in her fourth year of a five-year academic course studying law and I thought she might want to stay and complete it, but as soon as we talked about the States her eyes lit up and I knew she really wanted to go. We knew there were just more opportunities for dancers in the US, not to mention the fact that the new jobs we were being offered had a better salary than we were currently earning. Also, we were excited at the prospect of being coached by some of the world's finest dance tutors. A lot of the top European coaches chose to move to America.

Even though everything had been going well for me in Moscow, it felt right that we should at least try to grab the opportunity to go to the States and start a new chapter. It seemed foolish to ignore the prospect of more stability, more money, more opportunities for top-quality coaching, and then there was the lure of the lifestyle.

Since the Cold War, Russian propaganda had painted the US as somewhere that had fallen foul to all the worst excesses of capitalism. It was portrayed as a bad place, full of bad people. I think that Russians were scared of Americans, and vice versa. Yet for me the States had always seemed like a magical place. A lot of the music and movies I'd been influenced by growing up, like *Rocky*, had come from there. I'd grown up thinking that America was a superior nation, both economically and socially, and I was enchanted by the idea of experiencing it for myself.

I told my friend I would try to get a visa, even though I knew this would be very hard. We were aware that the statistics were against us – at the time, only 10 per cent of visa applications to Britain or America were accepted.

Anya and I went to the American Embassy, in September 2000, taking our papers with us. The authorities rejected our applications without ceremony, seeming not even to consider them. We were given a black stamp on our passports, which means you are not allowed to even apply to enter America for another five years.

Suddenly, we'd hit a roadblock: the choice had been taken out of our hands, or so it seemed. I didn't like the idea that I was being restricted from doing what I wanted. Usually, I view life philosophically and it would have been in character if I had just thought, Ah well, it wasn't meant to be, but for some reason in this instance I just couldn't let it go.

I went home and I fetched more documents – all the documents they could ever possibly ask for. Anya did the same, and, two weeks later, we were back at the Embassy. We waited in line to talk to an officer. Up first, I kept telling the officer that in making the decision not to grant us a visa to the United States he was destroying my dancing career. Something came over me at that point. I didn't raise my voice or become aggressive but I felt passionately that I wasn't going to take no for an answer. I remember saying, 'I'm not doing anything illegal, what more do you want from me?' Eventually, I think the officer either grew tired of having to listen to me or he recognised this wasn't a battle that he would ever win. He stamped my papers and granted me access to the USA.

In the meantime, Anya had gone up to the next window. Her officer had flat refused to consider her appeal for the same reason as before – she said Anya did not have enough documents. Anya began pointing at the window where I stood, saying, 'But they're letting *him* out and we are partners! You have to let me go too.'

At that point, the officer who had been dealing with Anya's application jumped out of her chair and ran over to the officer dealing with me to find out what was going on. We couldn't really understand what they were saying to each other because they were speaking in English, but what we did make out was that there was actually no reason for us to have our visas refused. All the paperwork was there and, because my officer had acknowledged this, Anya's had to do the same. A second later, Anya was having her papers stamped too, allowing her to accompany me to the States. A victory, I must tell you.

So, we were on our way to a new land. Instincts had told me it was the right thing to move to the US, and now my American adventure was about to begin.

It was November 2000, the day before Thanksgiving, when I finally set off for the USA. For some reason, all the way there I was terrified that I would be turned away from the country at the border. Even though I had all the correct documentation and the officers back in Russia had said it was fine for me to go, the experience of being refused on my first attempt at getting a visa had shaken me up. I was expecting some sort of last-minute refusal, some spanner in the works that would bring my journey to a halt, and it put me on edge.

Instinct had told me to do everything in my power to make sure I got to the States. Something within me felt that it was important. Despite the fact that I'd had regular work in Moscow and things were going well for me there, I had left behind everything that I'd worked for, but I instinctively knew in my gut that it was the right thing to do. I couldn't fall at the last hurdle. Of course, as it turned out, I managed to pass through the immigration at the airport without anything happening.

As soon as I stepped through the automatic door at the entrance to JFK, I knew I had found my real home. It's so strange, having lived in Russia pretty much all my life up until then, aside from the trips to Europe for dance competitions, that I immediately felt like I belonged in New York City. America and Russia are completely opposite, culturally, yet it took less than a minute before it didn't feel to me as if I had ever been a Russian person. Even the air somehow smelled familiar and the whole energy of the place felt really good; I was a New Yorker now.

Our friend Andrei came to pick us up at the airport, which is actually about a 30- or 40-minute drive out of the city, if there's no traffic. (I later learned that traffic is quite a big issue in New York.) I remember that he put on the radio as we were driving and I didn't understand a word the DJs were saying. My English was still very basic at that time but the main reason I couldn't understand them is that they seemed to be talking really fast – too fast for me to keep up. The traffic reports were especially difficult for me to try to understand. Rather than finding that daunting, I started to get really excited, imagining a time when I would be able to comprehend what was being said on the radio.

Euphoria took over. Even my friend's basic hire car was different to the cars we'd had back in Russia, being softer and grander. I decided it was the best car I had ever travelled in. As all the anticipation, adrenaline and pleasure swallowed me up, I started to feel as though I was riding along the highway on a huge cloud.

As we drove towards Manhattan, it was so surreal, so different and yet so familiar at the same time. The road itself wasn't like the roads we had in Russia; it was a proper highway, like I'd seen in films. Then all the tall buildings that make up the New York skyline came into view. Again, I'd seen the iconic image now in front of me in pictures and in lots of the movies I'd watched back home, but those images couldn't have compared to being there and seeing the real thing for myself.

Andrei lived in New Jersey, across the Hudson River. Even though he worked in Manhattan, it was cheaper for him to live out there. We stayed with him for the first couple of nights. From his place, he had the exact same view of New York as you see on the Miramax logo. It was night-time when we arrived and the whole city was illuminated. Even though it was November, it was still a lot warmer than it had been in Russia. To me, the climate was like summer time, even though it was actually winter.

My new studio in New Jersey, the Fred Astaire Studio, was owned by a couple named Charlie and Jeanie Penattello; we lived with them for three months while working there. I remember looking across the river from my new apartment and thinking I'd never seen anything like it in my entire life. Even though Moscow is a huge city, it is spread out across a much larger area than New York. There's a lot of empty space between the buildings; they're not all squished close together as in New York and they don't stretch up into the sky in the same way. Moscow has a lot of tall buildings but only about three of them that you could ever describe as 'skyscrapers' (at least when I was living there – there are tons of skyscrapers there today). My first impression of New York was that it looked like a massive neon hedgehog, with its twinkling spines reaching high into the dark night sky.

New York appeared to me really artificial, but incredibly alive at the same time – the vibe of the place gave it an authenticity that its architecture couldn't achieve on its own. You couldn't help but get swept up in the rhythm; everything was fast paced and exciting. Everyone seemed as if they were there to do something important. I threw myself headfirst into my new life and becoming part of that rhythm.

It would have been easy to feel overwhelmed but the momentum of being so busy with everything I had to do kept me going. I started teaching dance and trying to learn better English as I went along. At the beginning, as I was teaching dance, I'd point to a body part and whichever student I was working with would have to tell me what it was called. I'd say, 'Move your...' and they'd go, '...arm', and I'd store that bit of knowledge away, now knowing that bit was called an arm for the next time I needed to refer to it. It was like a trade-off – I was teaching them dance and they were teaching me how to speak their language.

Of course, I knew a little English when I left Russia. Most of what I had learned was picked up while competing in dance contests across Europe with the studio, though. All the coaches in the places I'd visited – Poland, the Czech Republic, Germany and Italy – would talk to their students in English. I'd also taken English classes at school but they hadn't really taught me much. During my oral exams, rather than ask me about specific things, my teachers would say, 'Let's just talk about anything, in English.' I would always end up speaking about a trip I'd taken to a dance competition, using broadly the same words and descriptions each time. Quite often, if I didn't know a word, the teacher would complete the sentence for me. They used to let us dancers off the hook from doing it properly because they knew how busy our training schedule was. Our studies, whatever the subject, always came second to the dancing.

Right at the beginning of my time in America, I was in a weird linguistic no-man's land, stuck between languages. My English dictionary hadn't kicked in yet, and my Russian one hadn't fully left me. The combined effect of learning a new way of speaking and the tiredness I felt from my super-hectic new schedule meant there were days when I would come home in the evening and simply forget how to speak at all! Anya and I got into the habit of speaking English to each other. Later, Anya went a little further than me and took English classes to get the proper American accent so that she could audition for acting roles.

I'd heard somewhere that, if you understand the words used in song lyrics, then you have really gotten to grips with a language. I reached that significant point very suddenly, I suppose because I was listening to music all the time while dancing. It was very exciting to listen to the songs I used to rehearse to back in Russia and to understand what they were really saying. It didn't affect how I danced, though; I simply found it exciting on a social level to finally grasp the meaning. At that stage, I wasn't yet proficient enough to put the meanings of the lyrics in the music I was dancing to into my movement, as I do now.

It took me about 18 months before I felt comfortable speaking in English to anyone I encountered and confident that I would understand what they were saying back to me. Today, it's become more instinctual for me to speak, think and even dream in English than Russian. A lot of my friends find bilingual people quite fascinating and want to know whether your inner monologue always remains in your mother tongue, no matter what you go on to learn afterwards. My experience is that it doesn't; my inner monologue is now English. Like that – *My inner monologue is now English* – I thought that in English, straight off!

One thing was for sure, as I began my new life amid the bright lights of this gigantic, glamorous city that I now called my home, I felt that, in more ways than one, the little startled bear who had fallen in love with dancing back in Siberia had come a long way.

Chapter 6

FOOD, GLORIOUS FOOD

While I was teaching in New Jersey, word worked its way round my students that I had another passion outside of dancing, and it was something they were keen to help me explore. This might seem at odds with your understanding of how dancers are and the strict regimes some of them use to stay in shape but I absolutely love food.

But it isn't just the chocolate I've already talked about that I adore; I'm into all kinds of food, from all over the world. While I was coaching, my students would bring me whole meals to class, just because I get so excited at the prospect of eating and I think they enjoyed seeing that pleasure register on my face. I remember I had one student, her name was Teri, and she must have been about 70 years old. She'd constantly be bringing snacks and chocolates to class. I was excited just to be there in the States, living my dream, but being given delicious, home-made food was another reason I used to look forward so much to teaching my lessons.

As I have already said, the first day after I arrived in the States, it was Thanksgiving. Charlie and Jeanie prepared us a huge feast. I had so little experience of food outside of what I was used to in Russia and Eastern Europe that, when someone told me that Americans traditionally put cranberry sauce on turkey for their Thanksgiving meal, I was very sceptical. I'd never even tasted turkey before, but I figured it must be a little like chicken and I couldn't imagine why you'd put a sweet sauce on top of that. I was even more confused when they told me that dessert was cheesecake! Though I was familiar with the concept of 'cheese' and again with that of 'cake', put the two words together and I just couldn't work out what this dessert could possibly be. Yet I tried, and loved, absolutely all of it and now cheesecake is one of my favourite desserts.

Today, I'm very adventurous with my choices in food. As long as it's not still moving, then I will try it! There's very little I won't sample at least once. I think this dates back to growing up in Russia and the strong flavours they use in the native cuisine. What they lacked in variety and freshness because of rationing, they made up for in potent flavour combinations. I remember someone telling me about an episode of the British reality show *Come Dine With Me*, where one of the contestants was originally from Russia. Apparently, the voiceover guy was talking as if she was crazy to put together some of the foods that she did. But the way I see it, all the meals in Russia are so hearty and flavoursome that, afterwards, you get a taste for adventure and you're not scared to try any dish that might come your way!

On the rare occasions when I get the chance to go back home to Russia to visit family, I always order *borsche*, which is a very popular, traditional Russian soup. It's a lot thicker, probably closer to a stew in texture, and has more ingredients in it than the soups you get elsewhere in the world. My mum used to cook it for us all the time when we were little. The soup always contains beef broth, potatoes, cabbage and beetroot, and then people will add different vegetables and seasoning on top of those basic ones to give the dish its distinct character. I've never tasted any that's as good as my mum's, though, even in the best restaurants.

In Eastern Europe, where I used to travel mainly for dance competitions before I moved to the States, the kitchens were very similar to those at home in Russia. A Polish meatball is still one of my top treats. For health reasons, I try not to eat too much meat on a day-to-day basis, but I cannot resist a Polish meatball!

My favourite things to eat depend on where I am in the world. There is at least one dish that I love in every single place I have visited throughout my lifetime, although, if I had to choose, I'd say that the best food I've ever eaten has been in Australia. Everything I tasted there was organic and fresh. It didn't matter where I ate or how much money it had cost me, it all tasted amazing because the quality of the ingredients was so good.

I think that the foods of a region tell you a lot about the character of that particular place. The cuisine also tells you something about the personality of the people. I know it sounds a little crazy, but I do think there is a correlation between the character of the food you eat and how you behave, and I know

I'm not the first person ever to believe this. There's a certain school of thought that says if you eat a lot of spicy food then you end up with a fiery temper, heated just like the meals you are consuming. I think they might be on to something.

For example, in Japan, a lot of the people are workaholics. They eat a lot of raw food that takes very little time either to prepare or digest. It's clean, quick and precise, just like the way of living out there. Then take South America. They feast on fried chicken and potatoes, which by contrast take a long time marinating to pack the flavours in and a great deal of time to break down and digest after you've eaten. In the same way, the people there are a lot more laid-back. They move and even speak more slowly than other cultures, as if they have all the time in the world.

In Italy, the food tends to be prepared with the philosophy that more than five ingredients are too much for one dish: everything is very simple. That tells me that Italian people are able to take pleasure in simple things and derive joy simply from living.

My first experience of Italian food was out at a restaurant when I was living in Moscow. It was someone's birthday and to celebrate we dined at an Italian restaurant. I had been so intrigued to try Italian food and remembered how different it was to what I'd been used to at that time. So, when I arrived in the US and everyone was discussing where we should go and eat, they dropped in the name of the particular restaurant I'd been to in Moscow and I got very excited. When we arrived there, it turned out to be a fast-food chain with the same name – Pizza Hut! In Moscow, Pizza Hut had been an actual five-star Italian restaurant and it had nothing to do with the fast-food chain with franchises all over the world, so I was a little disappointed.

Funnily enough, the food was the one thing I didn't immediately love about New York – to me, a lot of it seemed as if it was made of plastic. Ingredients like tomatoes and cucumber were nowhere near as nice as they had been in Russia. Having said that, before arriving in the States, I could have counted on one hand the number of times I had ever dined out at a restaurant and suddenly it seemed as if I was eating out all the time. I learned that New Yorkers don't tend to sit at home: they're always out, either working or socialising, maximising on the time they have in any given day. And the food is fast because it matches the pace of the city, so I guess that makes sense.

When I'm in Britain, I have a soft spot for shepherd's pie. I have a friend called Wendy Johnson, who is actually from New Zealand but maybe because she is used to cooking with lamb she makes the most incredible shepherd's pie. I suppose in some ways the dish reminds me of home – the combination of ground meat and potato is very much like a meal that Russians would eat – although we wouldn't layer them in the way British people do. It's putting one ingredient on top of the other in a pie format that makes shepherd's pie distinctly English. Because Russians would instinctually keep the meat and potatoes apart, marrying them in this way seems a little quirky to me, just like the British people who are quirky by nature.

In LA, everyone is very fixated on health, just as the cliché goes. What isn't true is the myth that LA people don't eat; they do eat a lot but it's all fresh and raw, and really good for you. Los Angeles is a place that is very focused on what is outside of a person and everything they eat has some sort of benefit in enhancing their physique in some way. I don't always think that's necessarily a bad thing, to think about your health and how what you're putting in your body will affect you.

The best thing I found about Western food culture was the fact that food places were open so late. In my profession, quite often I won't finish work until late at night. In the big cities like New York, Los Angeles and London, I still have access to every world cuisine, however late I might leave the studio. That means I get to indulge both my professional and personal passions, which is a wonderful thing.

The way I view things, one day I will get really old and I won't be able to dance any more but my love affair with food is something that can last a lifetime.

Chapter 7

BECOMING AN AMERICAN

The Fred Astaire Studio was in a New Jersey town named Ridgewood – a small, but beautiful place. Charlie and Jeanie were the studio owners and, apart from them, the only permanent residents were their daughter, Christina, a couple of other dance instructors, Anya and me. We spent a lot of time together but didn't tend to venture that much into the main parts of New York because we were quite limited, both in time and transportation. It was hard to find the time or energy to either plan or undertake a trip out of Ridgewood to explore the city.

Most of the other dance instructors I came into contact with at Fred Astaire Studios were Russian, Polish or Ukrainian. I was learning English from my students, and Anya and I would also speak English to each other as a faster way of picking up the language. After a while, when other coaches spoke to us in Russian, it began to feel weird.

I was still with Anya, both romantically and as a dance partner, and was spending almost all the tiny amount of free time I had with her. We were also hanging out a lot during competitions and shows, as well as when we were coaching and rehearsing. So, even though I technically met a lot of new people during this time, I can't say that I was really making any new friends in the way I would define the word. I didn't become close to anyone new.

On the one hand, my environment in Ridgewood was very tranquil in comparison to the time I spent in Moscow; on the other, I was so busy that everything became a whirlwind. I was trying to get new clients to teach at the studio; also to work on getting the correct paperwork so that Anya and I could become permanent residents in the USA, as well as learning a new language, so that really didn't leave much time at all for socialising.

Everything was so hectic that it wasn't until eight years later that I first got the chance to go back and visit my family in Russia. I was speaking to my mum every Sunday by arranging for her to use the landline in her neighbour's apartment. She did not have a phone of her own at the time.

I realised that, without my ever really noticing, I had become an American in terms of my life philosophy. I was so acclimatised to the culture over in the US that, to me, everything in Russia now seemed completely alien. Now I felt like a tourist, and not in a good way; I was completely outside of my comfort zone, unable to comprehend the way the people were, their attitudes and the lifestyles they led.

I'd go to the bank, or to the store in my hometown in Russia and the people behind the counter wouldn't even smile to acknowledge me. They were completely stony-faced. Certainly, they wouldn't greet me with 'Hi, how are you?' as everyone does in the States. In Russia, everyone seemed somehow closed in, as if they didn't want to talk to you and they'd prefer it if you weren't there. I just couldn't get my head round that mentality anymore. What had once been my normal now seemed to me miserable and impolite.

Also, I couldn't relate to the things that Russian people complained about anymore. Russia still hadn't quite settled into democracy; the country was now living in a capitalist regime but most of the people still had a communist mindset, like a hangover from the way the country had been so many years previously. So, Russians would moan about the government making decisions without first consulting the people to ask what they thought, or the fact that jobs and housing were no longer automatically provided for every citizen. These things just seem normal in Western society, and I'd spent so long living in America that it seemed obvious to me that they would be done in this way; I couldn't understand what people were so upset about.

Suddenly, Russians had to pay for such things as their education, healthcare and accommodation themselves. It made them very bitter. I observed that a lot of the Russian people spent their time trying to blame other people or organisations for everything that went wrong in their lives; I got the impression that everyone just felt a little bit sorry for themselves.

Of course, I viewed capitalism very differently to the people I spoke to back in Russia. I saw it as a friend, rather than the enemy. The way I saw it, I had the freedom to do whatever I wanted, and that was enough to put a permanent smile on my face. In Russia, I was regarded as if there was something wrong with me for thinking in that way. Over there, the beginnings of democracy were not greeted with my level of enthusiasm because, along with it, there were a lot of job losses and uncertainty about the future. When it came down to it, people were really frightened and that gave them a spiky, confrontational energy.

I remember listening to my dad complain about the state of the country and so I asked him, 'Why don't you start your own business?' but he simply waved away my suggestion, making some excuse about it being a lot of paperwork. For me, that kind of summed up the Russian mentality.

My relationship with my father has always been a little fraught and strange. He has always seemed distant, both physically and emotionally, to me. I found out much later in my life that my parents had actually divorced when I was five years old and my father had moved away. I don't remember it too well but I guess I must have thought he was away on a business trip at the time. A year later, he came back to my mum.

I do remember the day that my dad came back, when I was six. I was playing in the street outside our apartment complex when I saw him. He was wearing a military backpack and he reached into it to pull out a Rubik's cube, which he gave me. After that, he continued to live with us, even though I now know that my parents were legally divorced.

Looking back on the nine years that followed, I remember my parents were always arguing about something. When I was 15, my father moved out again for the second and final time. He lived with my grandma for a while. Later, he found another partner and still lives with her now. Of course, by that point, I was no longer living at home so it didn't have much of an impact on me. I remember my mum being really upset by the second split, but I told her that they clearly hadn't been happy together, so from my perspective it was a good thing that they should separate. My mother has not remarried but, if she met another man, I would be happy for her, as long as she was happy.

Since then, I haven't really had much of a connection with my father. He certainly never exercised any authority over me, or my decision-making. It was always Mum that I would telephone whenever I needed any opinion or permission to do something. I didn't need his support, so for that reason we didn't have much of a relationship and still don't to this day, although I do call him from time to time.

It took going back to Russia, speaking to my father and other people I used to know, to make me realise the extent to which I'd become immersed in American culture. I was, in every sense, a citizen of the United States.

Chapter 8

AT THE CENTRE
OF THE UNIVERSE

It wasn't long after I moved to the States that Anya and I were invited to join another studio, right in the centre of Manhattan, in Times Square.

The owners of Dance Times Square studio were a couple named Tony Meridith and Melanie La Patine. We became a part of their permanent staff. They were renting studio space to their friend, Vibeke Toft, and her former dance partner, Allan Tornsberg, would occasionally drop by. As a young man back in Russia, Vibeke and Allan had been two of my dance idols, which made it impossible to refuse the new position working alongside them, even if I had wanted to. Both Anya and I viewed the opportunity to work every day next to people I perceived as dancing legends as irresistible and incredibly exciting.

Back in Siberia, our coach Irina had made us watch videotapes of Vibeke and Allan, along with other famous ballroom dancers from their era. She did this so that we could try to establish what our own style of movement was. We would copy little bits of their routines and incorporate them into our own choreography. We'd sit and watch VCRs of their back catalogue of performances, rewinding them endlessly until we had incorporated the flavour into our own dancing.

I remember so distinctly watching Vibeke and Allan and learning parts of their dance routines, back in those days. My first memory of Vibeke was seeing her come out onto the dance floor with a huge fruit installation on her head to dance a Samba and thinking, Wow, this woman is amazing!

The first time I saw Vibeke teach at my new studio, I was completely star-struck. Allan tended to travel around a lot so she was at the studio on her own. It's rare for me to be so overwhelmed by seeing anyone – I tend to regard people as people, no matter what their status – but, with her, I was so nervous and shy. In the end, she had to come over and say 'hi' to me to break the ice. She was so casual about it, not pretentious in the slightest. It wasn't long before we all became friends.

It was incredible to have the opportunity to take lessons with these legends of dance pretty much any time I wanted. Their dance styles were very close to my own (which I suppose they would be since they'd influenced me so much growing up). In their style of dance, the woman is extremely feminine and the man is very strong. The man leads and determines where the dance will go next; he is the rhythm of the music and the woman is the melody, making the dance look pretty.

Working with Vibeke, Allan, Melanie and Tony, however, I realised that a lot of the techniques I knew up until that point were wrong. I suppose where Irina hadn't had a background in ballroom, it was inevitable that I would establish a few bad habits. Vibeke used our time together to break down my old habits so I could build myself back up to the same level again but this time as a better dancer technically. I always think of it as being like the story of the Three Little Pigs: before I'd built my dance foundations on straw and wood, but this time I was building them in stone.

In my previous studio, I'd been in peaceful New Jersey. Here, I was right in the centre of the action. Even if you have never been to Times Square, you will have seen it in countless movies and pictures. It's completely iconic and people flock there from all over the world, just to get a glimpse.

Times Square is pretty awe-inspiring. It was named Times Square because that's where the headquarters of *The New York Times* newspaper are situated. A massive commercial inter-section, it is always alive with activity. Huge neon billboards stretch high into the sky. Leicester Square in London is similar in some ways, although a pale imitation of Times Square, which is bigger and brighter, but also gaudier.

All the tourists who flock to New York City inevitably want to spend some time in Times Square because it is so famous. Because of that, more than any other part of New York, this is the place where the working people of Manhattan and tourists collide. According to Wikipedia, 39 million tourists come to Times Square each year and 300,000 people pass through it every single day. Times Square has famously been described as 'the centre of the universe'. I always saw it as a crossroads where people from different worlds collide.

For a big city like New York to function, 95 per cent of the population live like worms in a can, constantly wriggling about in a confined space. Native New Yorkers barely acknowledge each other as they hurry to work – and that's if they're in a good mood! On some days, they'd be swearing and shouting at each other as they marched on with the daily grind, so preoccupied with whatever was happening in their day. I quickly became used to being part of the swarm. After all, I was one of the people who was there all the time. I wasn't visiting, so I wasn't wrapped up in the mystery and sheer wonderment of the place anymore because it had simply become where I worked every day. Now I was in a hurry to get where I was going, dashing between the subway and where I had to be, just like everybody else.

I started to wish the crowds would move along faster because they were blocking my way to work. Now I would look at other people and label them as tourists; even though many were Americans and I was the one from Russia, it didn't feel that way. Damned tourists! I caught myself thinking on a couple of occasions. You know somewhere has truly become your home when all the tourists meandering around begin to annoy you on days when you are running late for work!

New York started to feel less extraordinary and breathtaking, and simply became the place where I lived.

I did try New Year's Eve on Times Square on a couple of occasions. It's meant to be the ultimate way to spend that particular holiday. People would come at three or four in the afternoon and stay all the way through until midnight. But for me I was just returning to work on a day off! I do remember one New Year's Eve when some of the contestants from season three of *So You Think You Can Dance* were invited to perform on a television show that was filmed on Times Square and I came along with them. We were on a balcony overlooking the crowds below. It was pretty cool, seeing it from that perspective. High in the neon skyline, there was a sense of magic. It reminded me why perhaps people would travel all that way and wait for so long to experience it.

Having said how ordinary New York eventually became, I can't say I ever lost the sense of being in the middle of everything. Working in Times Square, you really do feel as though you are in the 'centre of the universe'. In a whirlpool, the water always travels fastest at the centre, and New York, with its hustle and bustle and the crowds, which, if you're not careful, can sweep you along in whatever direction they are headed, felt to me as if it definitely had to be the centre of some big, global whirlpool. Even though the city had stopped feeling out-of-the-ordinary, it still seemed like the most important place on earth. While I was no longer wandering around completely enchanted by my new home as I had been at the beginning, I never lost the sense of excitement just to be a cog in the New York machine.

Even at the very beginning, I didn't do the usual sightseeing activities, though. I think, because I have been so used to moving around for my entire life, it's made me very adaptable and flexible to my environment; I settle in and call somewhere home very quickly. It's a good thing because it means I don't take a long time to establish my day-to-day life in a new place. I never feel anxious either anticipating or undergoing change; instead, I concentrate on the job at hand and getting on with what I have to do.

On the flip side, though, it does mean that the wonders of the world that other people enthuse about – like the Empire State Building, for example – I just haven't taken the time to go and see. Usually, I've been too tired after a day of intense training.

I remember we had a dance competition in a hotel on the ground floor of the Twin Towers in August 2001, but I didn't take the opportunity to go all the way up to the top to take in the view, like some of the others did, and, of course, in September 2011, they were blown up. I guess it just doesn't appeal to me to spend my time looking at buildings and statues. If I do have the energy to go out and explore a place, I prefer speaking to the people to learn what it's really like from them.

However it happened, I got used to both the good and the bad aspects of New York life incredibly quickly and for that reason I stopped noticing them. Generally, though, I was happy with my life there. For the first time, demand for my services was actually more than I could handle. Making the transition to the States had been great for my career, I had my health and, on the rare occasions when I did get some time off, I had a ready-made group of friends from the dancing circuit to have food and fun with.

In 2004, Anya and I broke up. In Russia, circumstances had thrown us together, but in New York we had more freedom and it put our relationship in a new light. We began to drift apart and we got to the stage where we both knew it was not working. It was a very friendly break-up and we continued to dance together and remained a big part of each other's life.

As well as working at the studio, I was working with my own private clients and regularly taking trips for dance contests throughout the United States and sometimes to Europe. I didn't know it at the time but during one of those trips, to the Puerto

above left: Four months old, and I am alive and happy.

above right: Aged two celebrating my birthday. I love cats and they love me... most of the time!

below: My father served in the Navy and I used to dress up in his hats. This is me, aged four, with my mum posing for our pictures.

This photo was taken in 1988 just after my brother, Sasha, was born.

Above and below: Family portraits: Mum, Sasha, my father and me. The first
picture also had has my grandma Lidia in it, too.

Monkeying arour
Six years old on the Black S
with my first dance partn
Actually, that monkey was v
mean to me and, after taking t
picture, it pulled my ha

In 1994, I left my parents' house and moved to Kemerovo with my dance studio.

Above: My dance studio Fiesta after a concert. We are dressed in Russian costumes.

Below: Outside in the park next to the art centre in our Latin costumes.

I made some great friends at the dance studio; we were like a little family.

Above: 14 years old in Novosibirsk. From left: Oksana, my dance partner at the time, Den, Lena, Aleksandr, me and my first dance teacher, Sergei Pushkov.

Below: During one of the competitions in Kemerovo in 1996.

nya moved to my dance studio when I was 16 and soon became my dance
rtner, and, four years later, we started dating. Knowing Anya shaped the
urse of things to come for me.

ove left: After one of the regional dance competitions in 1996. At that time,
Russia, it was popular to present finalist with gadgets like TVs or refrigerators!

ove right: Anya and me in 2004 after a dance competition.

low: Me and Anya performing a Latin dance.

Anya and I moved to the US together which ultimately led me to *So You Think You Can Dance*. Being on the show opened my eyes to a completely new world. This photo was taken on a rooftop in LA for the first show.

Rico, something happened that would shape the course of everything to come.

It's really easy, with the benefit of hindsight, to recognise the events in your life history that went on to shape your life. Most of us can pinpoint just a handful of key moments that have happened in our lives so far that kicked us into a different direction. It could be something as small and insignificant-seeming as missing a train, like the movie *Sliding Doors*. You might miss the train but you end up bumping into someone who introduces you to an experience you never thought you'd have. Or you could take a different route home from work and happen to spot an advertisement for the job of your dreams. Or you might meet your future partner because you decided not to go to the bar where you hang out every Friday night but try something new instead. Generally, it's the little decisions that turn out to be the ones that really matter in the end. It's funny how usually they also turn out to be the ones we spend the least time mentally ruminating over. That's part of the reason I believe so strongly in going with your instinct.

We rarely know at the time that what we are experiencing will mould the course of things to come. Most often, we see these situations as stumbling blocks, something that interrupted the path we were headed down before. If we're intent on continuing down the original path, then that's exactly what they become: a nuisance and a waste of time that briefly diverts us as we travel along our life's journey. Like I said, I've never been someone who plans too far into the future, though, so for me any little thing can be the catalyst for a total life reformation.

Sometimes, our course is determined by something huge and life altering, though. Either it changes your perspective, or it will force you to live differently from before. These are things like being in an accident, or more often than not an illness. Something that reminds you that you are human and you are mortal and the time we have on this planet is actually incredibly short.

In my case, it was an illness that transformed everything I'd known up until that point. The funniest thing is I have never been someone who likes to create drama or makes a fuss about things. At the time, I was so relaxed about the situation that I couldn't see it would turn out to be one of my life moments. I could never have known how significant it would be.

If I had not become sick, then I would never have ended up on television. And you probably wouldn't have heard of me and, almost certainly, I wouldn't be writing this book. I didn't realise I wanted fame because of my brush with death or anything as dramatic or predictable as that. In fact, I can't say the experience changed my perspective on things much at all but it undoubtedly began a chain of events that propelled me towards where I am today.

Here is what happened.

So, if you remember, at this point in my life, I was working in New York City and the bulk of my work was coming from giving ballroom classes to private students. Margaret was one of my clients. We always got along really well and I still keep in touch with her and visit her whenever I am near where she lives in the United States. She is of Chinese origin but she has lived in New York for a very long time. Margaret has never told me her age – she says it's a woman's prerogative not to reveal that information!

At the time, she and I were competing as a couple in a dance contest that was taking place in Puerto Rico. The idea behind this type of competition is that it forces those who really want to master the art of dance to up their game. Amateurs dance with professionals and this encourages them to push themselves and improve their dance skills. The combination of dancing with a professional and competing against each other pushes the amateur dancers to the next level.

My memories of that trip are really hazy and I only remember a very few things. I remember being struck by how beautiful Puerto Rico was; I also recall eating oysters one evening, and waking up in my hotel room the next morning with a high fever and feeling that I could not move. It was almost as if I had the beginnings of a cold but it felt different because of the heaviness in my limbs, which made it so hard to move. The symptoms had come on really suddenly. Boom! There I was, totally exhausted.

We stayed in Puerto Rico for five days and each day I grew increasingly sick. I came downstairs twice during my entire trip, both times to dance. The rest of the time was spent lying in my hotel bed. I remember that Margaret kept inviting me for dinner every night but this was the one time when I couldn't bring myself to think about food! Most of the time, I didn't even know where I was; I felt lost in time and space. I'd open my eyes and it would be light, then I'd open them again and it would be dark. Whole chunks of time were passing, literally with the blink of an eye.

I recall thinking that above all else I could not let my student down and somehow I made it down the stairs of the hotel to the ground floor, where the competition was taking place. In the end, Margaret and I made it through to the final heats, even though I was just going through the motions, gripped by a powerful malaise.

It's recommended usually that you don't dance when you have the flu. That's what I thought I must have, despite the fact that I didn't have any of the other symptoms, just this fever and overwhelming tiredness. Even though I knew I shouldn't, I still danced.

I've always had the attitude of 'the show must go on' and I'd danced with a cold before when there was no getting around it. Irina, my coach in Russia, used to say, 'There's only one reason why you can't show up for rehearsals and that's because you are dead!' I'd pretty much lived my career by this philosophy because that's what I grew up with.

Through sheer willpower alone, I managed to dance. The dancing took place all in one day during the trip. I remember stumbling downstairs and I was concentrating so hard that I couldn't even smile at all the people who were saying 'hi' to me as I put on my costume and got ready. At the time, I just didn't have it in me to muster the energy it would take to shape my face into a grin.

I don't remember much about how I got back to New York City. By that stage, everything was just so blurry it didn't seem real. However, I do recall taking a lot of aspirin before my flight to try to combat my symptoms. Later, I found out that doing that, combined with the altitude, was the worst thing I could have done in the circumstances and actually made my condition more serious.

Margaret's mum apparently used to do this thing where she would pinch the skin on the back of her neck and pull it, and the action was somehow supposed to relieve your ailments. For the entire four-hour flight, Margaret was doing that to me over and over again. It was so annoying, but she was only trying to help and I was powerless to resist.

I've flown a lot in my life, but this particular flight felt as if it would never end. I didn't know what to do with myself. I wasn't in pain exactly, but I didn't have the physical or mental agility to react to the things that were happening all around me. It was as if nothing really existed. I don't remember getting from the airport to my apartment at all – I know I must have caught a cab to make the journey, but it passed in one big haze.

Anya was really shocked the first time she saw me back in the States. She said she had never seen me look so sick. We were broken up at this stage, but she would come and visit me every day. I stayed in my apartment while she went out to get me medicines and chicken soup. At that point, we were still working on the basis that I had some kind of flu. None of the medicines Anya brought me worked. As the hours passed, I wasn't getting any better; in fact, my condition was growing worse and worse.

Despite all of this, I wasn't panicking. I have never babied or felt sorry for myself when in the grips of an illness. Once, while living in Moscow, I flew to North Siberia for a show and didn't wear a hat to help protect me from the freezing temperatures, so, of course, I got a ridiculous cold. That was probably the most sick I had ever been up until what happened in Puerto Rico. I had to spend a day in bed but the very next day I was back to dancing again. That's the normal kind of dance mentality.

People never stopped working when they got sick back in Russia, because the thinking was 'we all get sick, stop feeling sorry for yourself and do what you have to do'.

I think growing up without having parents around all the time played a part in the way I viewed illness as well. My mum was never around to tell me to stay home from school, or to call a doctor out when I was young. I'd grown used to soldiering on, so it never occurred to me to seek help once I got back to New York.

It was Anya who was the first person to say, 'I don't think this is the flu', and she called an ambulance. By that point, I was so delirious that all I could think of was how exciting it was to ride in an ambulance. To add to the experience, I asked the paramedics to turn the sirens on. I was like a little boy again, unable to think of any possible consequences or implications.

When we arrived at the hospital, I was taken into a room and questioned about my symptoms. I lay with my hot head on a cool desk in the emergency room as the doctors fired questions at me. They asked how much discomfort I was in on a scale of one to 10. I told them 12! They laughed and gave me some pills for a cold. Because of my symptoms – a stiff neck, feeling tired, weak and feverish – they must have assumed I was exaggerating.

The next day, I was even worse. Again, I found myself at the hospital. This time, I wasn't greeted with much urgency or enthusiasm. They might as well have said, 'Oh, *you* again!' I know I must have seemed ridiculous to them – a grown man who kept coming back to the emergency room for what they thought was a common cold, something every human being experiences.

They gave me papers to fill in and I was told to wait, which

I did for two or maybe three hours. I went in for a routine scan, just to be sure. Different people were coming into the room to talk to me and to tell me what was about to happen next; none of them seemed too concerned.

All of a sudden, three doctors came rushing into the room and said they needed to get me into a ward fast. Anya started freaking out because of the urgency with which they were speaking and moving. She knew my condition had to be more serious than any of us first thought.

It turned out that I had developed a condition called Lemierre's Syndrome. It's extremely rare and difficult to diagnose because it usually affects young, healthy adults. I was told that you get it if you work too hard. Your immune system crashes from not taking care of yourself or getting enough rest, then what was a sore throat develops into an abscess. In layman's terms, all my saliva had begun collecting in a pocket at the side of my throat and this in turn caused me to have a blood clot in my neck. The reason the doctors had to react so fast was that the blood clot was now travelling towards my brain!

I knew enough to know that if the blood clot reached my brain it would be the end for me: instant death.

It was November 2006 when I was admitted to hospital. For the next three weeks, my body became like a pincushion, constantly full of needles. I had two drips in each arm, which were changed hourly, giving me intravenous antibiotics to try to build my immune system back up again. Eventually, the blood clot dispersed and disappeared.

Being in hospital was the least active I can ever remember being for my entire lifetime. I went from teaching for 10 hours and rehearsing for three or four hours every day to suddenly being a sick person. I just sat in my hospital gown, watched a lot of television, played computer games on my PSP and tried to eat things. I remember being so weak that even getting up to have a walk along the hospital corridor would mean I'd have to lie down afterwards. I lost a lot of weight and for the first time ever I grew a beard. I must have looked like a little goat, sitting in that hospital bed.

When you lose the strength in the muscles that you've grown so used to having, it makes you think. Before I got ill, I would see old people shuffling along the street and think, Why can't you move faster? Now, I have more empathy for those who have diminished capacity for whatever reason. I know how quickly muscles lose their strength and tone, and how much time it takes to build them back up. As it turned out, for me it was at least six months before I returned to full fitness.

My students and friends visited me in the hospital and brought me food to try to tempt me to sustain my weight. I don't remember ever freaking out as much as they were. Everyone seemed so scared that I had almost died and by the possibility that it still might happen. I can't say I ever thought about that, really – I guess I went into self-preservation mode, not allowing myself to be frightened because I simply had to concentrate on getting better.

When I was discharged from hospital after two weeks and returned home to my apartment, I was too weak to work. I spent a month just struggling to get well again. My immune system was still so fragile that whenever I went outside, even if it was just for a few minutes, I'd catch a cold. Anya used to yell at me for going out at all. She thought I should stay in, but all I could think was that I had to build my strength up because I had to get back to work and pay my bills. I kept testing myself – going to the store, or for a walk around the block. Because of the nature of what I do, I'm always partially self-employed. If I don't work, I don't get paid – there's no such thing as sick leave.

By February 2007, I was doing a little better and even going back to work a bit, but nothing like on the scale that I had been dancing before. It was March when Anya said to me, 'Pasha, I do not know how long it will take you to get better, but there's a show auditioning in town and I really think while you're not working full time we should go for it.'

The show was called *So You Think You Can Dance*.

Chapter 9

SO YOU THINK
YOU CAN DANCE?

From the earliest moments of her learning about the show, Anya was totally fixated on the idea of the two of us auditioning for Fox Broadcasting's *So You Think You Can Dance*.

While out walking one day, she had spotted the lines of people waiting outside a theatre in Times Square. She'd been curious as to what all the hundreds of people were queuing for and found out that they were all hoping to try out for the show. Usually, we wouldn't have had the time on our hands to even think about trying out for something like that, but because of everything that had happened with my illness she figured the timing was perfect and that we should go for it.

I was vaguely aware of *So You Think You Can Dance*; indeed, it was hard not to be if you lived in the United States where it is an institution, but my interest really didn't go beyond that. Television had always been more of an ambition for Anya than for me – I never planned to be on people's screens and dive into that world. At that time, it just didn't factor into my thinking.

When Anya suggested that we should audition for *So You Think You Can Dance* the first time, I flatly refused. After being in hospital and all the effort it had taken for me to get my strength back, I felt that my life was finally getting on track once more. I was back at Melanie and Tony's studio teaching again and at last I was able to venture outside without getting colds every time I left the house. Things were moving in the right direction after what seemed like a very long time.

At that stage, all I was trying to do was to get my old life back, the one I had before I went into hospital. I'd liked that life. I felt as I did when I travelled to New York from Russia: I'd been given everything I ever wanted and then all of a sudden it had been snatched away from me by my illness.

Anya, on the other hand, was determined that we should audition for the show. She kept bringing it up and nagging non-stop. She said she couldn't audition on her own because she is a ballroom dancer and, in order to do that style of dancing, she needed a partner. Eventually, she managed to talk me into at least coming along with her to the auditions. I didn't want to try out for the show myself but I said that I would go with her for moral support and to watch. I suppose in the back of my mind I was thinking that I'd partner her if she needed me to in order to show off her skill.

The first day we turned up to the open auditions at the Manhattan Center theatre on West 34th Street, they were full to capacity and they weren't letting any more people in. My attitude was 'oh well, it obviously wasn't meant to be'. There was a part of me that was relieved about that; now we could drop the idea.

Anya wasn't resigned to fate in the same way that I was, though. She still wanted her audition so she asked some people from the show if she could come back the next day. Of course, I'd agreed that I'd be with her when she tried out and I was going to honour that promise, but I couldn't help but be annoyed that coming back the next day meant another day when I wouldn't be able to work. Another day I would lose money. Another day that made it even less likely that I would be able to pay my rent that month.

We came back to the same theatre where the auditions were being held the next morning. Anya was given a big sticker with a number on it. Already I'd told her that I didn't want to dance if I could possibly help it and I was just there to support her and to see what the other dancers were doing, which would be interesting.

So You Think You Can Dance is a show that features all different types of dancing styles. I was looking forward to seeing some hip hop and jazz, and how people were going to interpret the traditional moves to try to stand out from the hundreds of others auditioning that same day.

There must have been around a thousand people who had all come to audition the day Anya and I were there. The huge crowd was divided into groups of 10 and those groups were going into a small room, one batch of 10 at a time.

We didn't know it right then but in the audition room stood Jeff Thacker, one of the producers of *So You Think You Can Dance* and absolutely notorious. He was working in television in the UK and the US, and has a reputation for being extremely harsh and demanding. He's British as well and I think the accent helps him to sound even more intimidating.

As I found out later, Jeff's job involves overseeing everything to do with *So You Think You Can Dance*, from the auditions to the live tour afterwards. On this particular occasion, he was there to pre-screen the dancers before a selection of them went on to audition in front of the judges you see on the television show. As those auditioning danced their hearts out in front of him, desperate for a shot at being on the show, Jeff would stand completely motionless. He had his chin down, his legs apart and his arms folded across his chest. There was absolutely no emotion in either his face or body as he assessed the dancers. It was impossible, from an outside perspective, to tell what he was thinking.

When Anya and I went into the little audition room, we found it was just a small room with a carpeted floor. I got the impression it was probably used as a meeting room the rest of the time. There was a tiny square – probably only three by three metres – of hardwood floor in the centre of the room and, one by one, the hopefuls were called up to dance on it. With only a few seconds to show Jeff exactly what they could do, they all had to dance to the same song, which I suppose was fair. This time it was Justin Timberlake's 'Sexy Back'.

A few years later, after I'd taken part in *So You Think You Can Dance*, I was invited to help Jeff with the pre-screening process I'm describing. I realised then how difficult his job must be. It's easy to spot the people who are either really, really terrible or completely amazing at dancing. But all those who don't fit into those two categories – the ones who are proficient and have a talent but aren't spectacular – well, after a while, they all start to look the same. It's similar to when you go shopping for some perfume or aftershave and you walk around the store smelling bottle after bottle of fragrance. After a while, you lose the ability to distinguish between scents.

Jeff's task was to spot potential. The thing about potential is that it's not always so immediately obvious as you might imagine, but he had an eye for it.

So You Think You Can Dance isn't just a show about dancing. It's as much about the personalities of the contestants. Some people had a loveable personality or an interesting background; others were really beautiful, or feisty. These are the people we know will make good television regardless of their dancing ability.

Some people bring an element of entertainment to the camera that has nothing to do with the way that they dance. Others manage to be kind of mesmerising when they dance and this has nothing to do with their technique. In the same way that some of the most popular musical performers are not necessarily the best technical singers, they just have that undefinable quality that makes people want to look at them. I guess it's not the fairest thing, but that's the world of show business for you. That's part of the reason I never wanted to be involved with television in the first place.

So, back to the audition room that day and Anya was the one being judged. I sat at the side of the meeting room, wearing jeans and a little tank top with a smirk on my face as I watched all the people trying so hard to impress Jeff. Anya's number was somewhere in the middle; she wasn't the first or the last to audition of her group of 10. When she was called up, she walked to the makeshift dance floor, planted her feet, tensed her body to find her core, stretched her fingers and gathered herself. She didn't even have to start on an actual dance move. She lifted one arm up, making to start her routine, danced just two counts of eight and Jeff cut her off by saying, 'Okay, thanks.'

Everyone else had been given a little longer to demonstrate what they were able to do; now, her audition was over in a blink and it would have been easy for her to be disappointed. But I had spotted something that Anya had not: as she prepared herself on the dance floor, for a split second I'd seen Jeff's mask slip and his jaw drop. Anya is an incredibly beautiful girl and even that simple gesture of limbering herself up had been intensely sexy, while making it clear she was a real professional. I knew she must be in with a chance, even if she herself did not.

Some numbers were called and told that they had made it through to the next round of auditions, others that they had been unsuccessful. Anya was told she had made it through, then Jeff looked over at me as I sat in the corner and asked if we were dance partners. He asked us to show him how we danced together. Even though I sort of knew where all this was going (and it wasn't in the direction I had initially intended), Jeff is not the sort of man you say no to. When he asks you to do something, you do it. So I joined Anya on the piece of hardwood floor and we danced two or three Latin moves, again to the tune of 'Sexy Back'.

When we were done, Jeff strode across to where we were standing until he stood just a couple of feet away from me. He looked straight into my eyes and said the words that would change the course of my career and my life forever...

'So, why aren't you auditioning?' asked Jeff Thacker, the steely British producer.

'I'm just here to help my partner,' I replied.

'Yes –' it was clear he understood that part '– but *why* aren't *you* auditioning?'

That was the part he didn't understand.

I told him I was tied up with work.

'Yes, but why aren't you auditioning?' he asked me for the third time.

It was clear that he didn't consider that I'd answered his question to a level he was satisfied with and now he was going to keep on asking it, in exactly the same way, until I did.

Wow, this guy's annoying! I thought to myself. Like a dog with a bone, he just didn't seem able to drop it – no matter what response I gave him.

Eventually, I stopped trying to be polite and simply said, 'I just don't want to do it.'

Jeff nodded and paused for a moment, drawing breath. Then he gave Anya and me the bottom line, delivered in a way only he possibly could.

'If you don't audition, I won't let your partner through. If you do audition, I will let you both through. Take it or leave it.'

He told us that we had the rest of the day to think about it and he was allocating me a number just in case I changed my mind and decided to go for it. They didn't have any new numbers left, though, so Jeff simply picked one up from the table of people who had already been selected to go through to the next round. I later found out that it was the number of a guy called Danny. He was a ballet and contemporary dancer who ended up being a finalist on that series of the show.

So, I had a number, an ultimatum and a decision to make. Whatever choice I was going to make, it would affect the rest of my life. It was like something out of a movie. Of course, I'd made big decisions before, like leaving the studio in Siberia and following Anya to Moscow, then leaving Moscow to head for the United States. This time it was somehow different. For what must have been the first time ever, my instinct wasn't telling me anything at all. It didn't seem obvious, natural or logical to do the show or *not* to do the show.

I knew if we made it through the live audition, which from Jeff's reaction it looked as though we were going to, it would mean training and more auditions in Vegas. It would mean leaving the New York studio and everything I had worked so hard for in the first place and rebuilt after my illness. Then again, I wasn't stupid enough not to recognise that this was an opportunity. It was something thousands of people dreamed of, and potentially a new and exciting adventure for me to embark upon. Plus, who knew where it would lead?

Then, of course, there was Anya to consider. She really, really wanted this and had made it obvious from the beginning. Even though we were no longer together as boyfriend and girl-friend, she was still one of my best friends. I loved her and I wanted to do the right thing for her career as well as mine. Also, I had to factor in the thought that kept popping up in my head: *If she hadn't called an ambulance a few months beforehand, I would probably have been dead.* I figured I probably owed her one for saving my life.

When I say I will do something, I like to commit to it fully. If I was auditioning for *So You Think You Can Dance*, I was going to give it everything I had. I would embrace the opportunity with both hands, and I had to be prepared mentally to take the competition all the way to its conclusion. All I had to do was figure out whether or not this was what I truly wanted. I was therefore certainly not taking this decision lightly and I had only a limited amount of time to make it.

After an entire night spent pondering my future, I was still no closer to being totally sure what I wanted. Being sick had shaken me up; the whole experience had made me realise what it's like to be out of work and without any access to employment. As they say, the more you work, the easier it is to get new prospects and clients; to build yourself up as a business from scratch is the hardest thing. I knew this from having to do it in Moscow. I thought it was probably prudent to hold on to the clients I'd built up so far in New York, and they wouldn't wait around while I went off to Vegas for a television show.

I also knew enough about *So You Think You Can Dance* to know that, if we did progress further and go on to compete in the live shows, it would mean relocating to Los Angeles. At that time, I'd been to LA on a couple of occasions and it had failed to impress me much. Later, I found out that I didn't know the city at all because I'd only ever seen the insides of hotels and LAX airport. Today, I am completely in love with LA, but at the time a feeling of not loving Los Angeles in the same way as I loved New York did factor into my thought process.

All night, I stayed awake thinking about what I was going to do. I even called some of my friends and asked them what they thought, which is out of character for me. Usually, my choices come from within, only this time I needed some outside guidance. All of my friends advised me to go for it. After being singled out by Jeff, they said I'd be absolutely crazy not to. They couldn't see that I'd be losing anything at all; they didn't think of it as taking a huge gamble in the way that I did.

In the end, I concluded it's always better to take an opportunity than to let it slide. All the circumstances seemed to be willing me to go for it and it was only my own doubts that were standing in my way. So, the next day, much to Anya's delight, we found ourselves at the televised auditions for *So You Think You Can Dance*.

Chapter 10

A WHOLE
NEW GROOVE

As it turned out, Anya's and my televised *So You Think You Can Dance* audition went on to receive thousands of YouTube hits within days.

Anya and I had turned up in just our rehearsal clothes; she was in a simple black jersey dress and I was wearing jeans and a black top. But it didn't matter that we were not wearing eye-catching costumes because the routine we chose to do really got the judges hot under their collars! We danced to a song called 'Magic Carpet Ride', a fast-paced number to which we did some Latin choreography. The moves we danced were very sexy. Everything emanated from the hips.

Afterwards, judges Nigel Lythgoe and Mary Murphy told us that the routine had been 'so hot' that we were the best ballroom dancers they had ever had on the show. Watching it back, I also know that, even before we really started to dance, the first thing that Nigel said about Anya was 'she is *so* sexy!' I guess that in bringing some sensuality to proceedings we were giving them what they wanted.

So You Think You Can Dance attracts dancers of all different abilities and calibres. You don't need to have had professional dance training to try your luck in getting a place on the show. Most of the people who audition are amateurs in the sense that they are not paid to dance, even though they have had some training, or they have another job as well as dancing, which they do only part-time. Anya and I had danced pretty much all day, every day since we were kids, and for that reason we were on a different level to most of the other people there. That's not to say we were any more talented on a fundamental level, but we'd definitely had more practice and performing came more naturally to us.

Also, we weren't suffering from the nerves that some of the other contestants were going through before they went in to audition on camera. We were used to being watched and judged after years and years of taking part in professional dance competitions. It was the perfect preparation for a show like *So You Think You Can Dance*. The audition process was like a home from home, really. We weren't fazed by any of it – at least not in those very early stages, anyway.

Anya and I were also aware that we were dancing a style that not many of the other contestants were exhibiting and that helped our chances. Most of the other dancers who had been put through to this stage of the process did hip hop, freestyle, ballet or jazz. I think purely for variety as much as anything else the odds of our getting through the auditions to the next stages were always going to be high.

The format of the show is such that there are three options you can be given after you have danced in front of the judges on camera. You can firstly be told that you have not been successful and you have to go home. Secondly, you can be told that you need a little more training, which the show supplies for you, to see if you can come back and dance better in a second audition. Or the third option is that you can be told that you are good enough to go straight through to the show's next rounds, which take place in Las Vegas.

'You're going to Vegas!' one of the judges will declare to the chosen dancers after a dramatic pause. The way it's expected that you will respond to this good news is to scream and jump up and down, or maybe cry because you're so overwhelmed. I remember, after Anya and I were told we were definitely going to Vegas, we left the audition room and the show's host Cat Deeley and the backstage crew came over to record our reaction. We had to be asked to go back to the door and come out again, this time acting more energetic and excited so that we were in keeping with the tone of the show.

In reality, we had been completely nonplussed by the judges' verdict, and I think that must have shown on our faces and in our body language the first time we exited the audition room. It wasn't that we weren't pleased and we did smile and high-five one another, but we didn't completely collapse or act crazy. This is partly a Russian thing; we're not prone to big public displays of screaming or to being over the top when it comes to showing our emotions. It's just not how we're wired to react to life.

Other contestants were hugging each other and crying while the cameras captured their reactions. Their response to the news that they were 'going to Vegas' was genuine, I think. They saw it as the biggest victory.

The way Anya and I viewed things, though, was that the competition was only just beginning. It was of course a good thing to have confirmation that we were competent dancers who had honed our skill. Of course we were grateful to have the opportunity to dance in a very public forum, but we hadn't really done anything challenging yet. It wasn't as if we'd won, so why would we jump around? Now we had to prepare ourselves for the real work to begin!

Both of us had sacrificed the lives that we knew to be there, so we were going to give it our very best shot. Already we were focused on round two.

So, I was on the move again, this time to the bright lights of Las Vegas, where I was about to face the most difficult audition of my career.

Chapter 11

VEGAS

My first real memories of Las Vegas were food related. Knowing me as you do now, it will come as no surprise that one of my favourite things about the city was the all-you-can-eat buffets in almost all of the hotels.

My first experience of an all-you-can-eat was at the MGM Grand Hotel and Casino. It was enormous – a whole room crammed with row upon row of different types of food from all over the world. I must have gone back at least 10 times altogether!

When I first arrived in Vegas, it was still only April 2001 and I had not been in the United States very long. By now, I'd been over in the US for less than six months and a lot about the culture was still new to me. I'd never ever been in an environment before where, for $20, I could eat as much as I wanted. I couldn't believe it, so I sampled everything they had to offer.

I began with some soup. Then I had four different kinds of fish, followed by meatballs with spaghetti. I then moved on to potatoes, lasagne and vegetables. Then there were the salads; I'd never known salads like it before. In Russia, the salads are very dense and heavy – even a salad has to be hearty and filling to protect you from the cold winters. The kind of 'salad' I had been used to contained eggs, potatoes, peas and pickles, and often chicken, ham or baloney (a type of sausage) in chunky cubes. Russian salads have names like 'ground cheese and garlic' or the famous 'mackerel in a fur coat', which was the dish the Russian lady made for the episode of *Come Dine with Me* that I mentioned earlier. Western salads were a whole new world of colour and taste.

I was also determined to try all the different types of salad dressing the MGM Grand had to offer and it seemed there were hundreds. That was a novelty. In Russia, we dress salads either with sunflower oil or with mayonnaise; there are no other options. So there I was, pouring all these different sauces over my food like a man possessed.

I went back to the buffet another two or three times to re-sample all the foods I had particularly enjoyed. I remember being so happy in that moment, just surrounded by endless amounts of gorgeous food.

It was a 10-minute walk from the MGM Grand with their amazing buffet back to where we were staying, at the Luxor on Las Vegas Boulevard South. I have never in my life been a slow walker, yet it must have taken me about an hour to get there. I was so full of food that I couldn't even walk properly! It was only after I stood up from the lunch table and tried to take a couple of steps that it suddenly dawned on me how much I had really eaten. I'd stuffed myself so tight there was no room for anything else, no movement of my joints and no air in my lungs!

I couldn't bend; I was walking by heaving the whole of my body from side to side in order to move forward. I had to walk like a cowboy – a swaggering, clammy, two-dimensional cowboy, sweating with each step he took. Anya was with me at the time, and I remember she gave up on me after a while and went on ahead because I was too slow! After that, I took it a little easier on the all-you-can-eats.

It's very hot in Vegas pretty much all year round, which pleased me because I'm in love with the hot weather. Some of the things I experienced in Siberia growing up may have given me very negative associations with cold weather, so today I'm happiest in the heat.

I remember as a young boy when I was still living with my parents, the heating in our apartment was controlled centrally by the town hall, so everyone's radiators in the whole town went on and off at the same time. There didn't seem to be any pattern to when they'd switch them on and off, from what I could work out. So, when you'd come in out of the freezing-cold outdoors, whether you'd find your radiators on or off seemed to me as if it was a matter of pure luck. My mum used to have to wedge cotton-wool balls into the gaps between the glass window frames and doors to stop the bitter winds from getting in the house. Then she'd soak sheets in soap and water, and lay them on top to keep the cotton-wool balls in place. Once the sheets dried, they would stick and stay there throughout the whole winter as insulation. Two winters ago, I was able to buy some double-glazing for my mum. It was a revelation to her!

The worst thing about growing up in Siberia, though, was that feeling of having to get out of your warm bed in the morning. I'm sure that's a feeling most people who've ever stayed in a cold climate can relate to – having to drag yourself out of the comfort of your bed on a winter's morning. Well, there's no other word for it: it sucks! In the grips of the Russian winter season, that feeling was magnified by a hundred. You needed to really want to get out of bed and start your day, which is why it was lucky I was dancing and doing what I loved from such a young age. So now, anything around 35 degrees, which some people (especially the British) might call too warm, is my kind of weather.

I didn't get to see that much of Vegas during my visit because the training for *So You Think You Can Dance* was so intense. We had only a matter of hours to learn new dance disciplines and prepare ourselves for the live shows, so this wasn't a vacation in any way but what I did manage to see of the city during that time I absolutely loved.

They have themed hotels on the main strip, which try to replicate different places around the world. So there is one that is dedicated to Paris, another to Rome, another hotel had an Egyptian theme, and so on and so forth. I thought it was a fantastic thing, being able to visit different countries around the world simply by crossing the road.

The hotel that's a tribute to Italy (Venice) has painted ceilings as a skyscape, complete with clouds, to give the illusion of being outside even though you are indoors. They also had a replica of the Eiffel Tower, just to the side of the main building. The MGM Grand, the hotel that was the scene of my first buffet experience, was themed around the MGM

Studios' mascot that you see at the beginning of movies. You probably know it – it features a lion roaring, so that hotel had real lions inside in a cage.

The Luxor, where we were staying, had an Egyptian theme. Outside was a copy of the Great Sphinx, and inside everything was in that style. Everywhere was painted in a golden, opulent palate, from the restaurant to the shopping area to the in-house nightclub. It was pretty cool!

I did discover a favourite Vegas hotel and it's one I return to every time I visit the city. It's called the Bellagio and they have these beautiful glass flowers everywhere and a fountain outside with a light show every 15 minutes. It was so spectacular to watch. The best thing about the Bellagio is that they have the most beautiful gardens, complete with a butterfly sanctuary. However, what impressed me most were the white, milk and dark chocolate waterfall installations on one of the walls, just like the Roald Dahl book about Willy Wonka and his chocolate factory. Imagine, for a chocolate addict like me, the effect that the sight of those waterfalls would have! Luckily for the hotel, the waterfalls were protected by a glass front or I might have been swimming in them.

Las Vegas is never ever quiet. Even more than New York, I recall that it was always alive with sounds. There's maybe two miles of the main strip with the hotels I am describing. It's a long, wide avenue complete with the main casinos that all the tourists want to visit. There is always a lot of traffic, no matter what time of day. People line the sidewalks, busking. They'd usually have a sound system and play instruments, usually a guitar, over the top. There are huge television screens along the strip that project commercials for the various shows you can go and see; they change every few seconds. Then there are real people in flamboyant costumes hanging around outside the hotels, talking to passers-by about the shows as human advertisements. There are feathers and sequins and bright, garish colours everywhere you turn. Walking along that strip is like being assaulted by a sea of colour, sound and activity. It's so loud and so overwhelming that you just don't know where to look first. Your attention is constantly caught by something bigger and brighter and louder than the last thing you saw.

The heat also makes the atmosphere feel kind of frantic. It isn't so much the temperature as the fact that the air stays completely still. Las Vegas is situated in a bowl – the land on all sides of it is raised so the air literally has nowhere to go. It's so hot that, if you leave your car outside by midday, you can fry steak and eggs on the hood. With no breeze to blow all that heat around, you feel as though you could literally cut the air with a knife. Getting from A to B in Vegas always involves smashing your way through a wall of people, air, heat, sound, colour and activity. Sometimes you have to psyche yourself up to do it. There's no such thing as a peaceful, leisurely walk out there.

When you step inside one of the hotel casinos, it's like a world within a world. They're always dimly lit so you have no concept of the passing of time – I think it's to encourage gamblers to spend longer in there playing the slots because they haven't realised how much time has passed since they came in. The casinos are air-conditioned and sound proofed so all you can hear inside is the noise of slot machines. It's sort of a sanctuary from the chaos outside, but not really because the world behind the doors of the buildings is just as artificial and insane.

In a way, this new adventure – the one I was embarking on with *So You Think You Can Dance* – was mirrored by the feeling you would have of slipping between worlds if you walked in and out of hotels along the Vegas strip. I was there to dance and, from that point of view, the experience should have been familiar but it wasn't like anything I'd ever known. Nothing could have prepared me for the challenges the show had planned. It was fruitless to fight it, I just had to surrender myself to this part of the journey and smash my way through that wall.

Chapter 12

'YOU HAVE
TO FEEL IT'

I believe that part of the point of the Las Vegas training section of *So You Think You Can Dance* is to test the mental strength and stability of the contestants.

Taking part in a reality show like that, especially if you're not used to being in an environment where you are under the scrutiny of cameras all the time, eventually takes its toll on absolutely anyone. You go through such extreme highs and lows, you are physically and emotionally exhausted, but you also get all these rushes of adrenaline and euphoria, so it's like being constantly on a rollercoaster. You have to be prepared for and able to deal with all of that, because it's only going to intensify once you get to the live shows.

The way that *So You Think You Can Dance*'s producers would test us and make sure we were up to the challenge was by taking us out of our comfort zone and throwing unexpected challenges our way, ones that we had to deal with quickly. They'd rehearse us until we were ready to drop and then tell us we had to create a routine in a group with some other dancers to show the next morning. We'd then be sleep deprived in addition to everything else that was going on. We were learning new styles of dance over a really short period of time, too. It sounds as if it was a harsh thing to put us through, but it has to happen that way: if we were unable to handle everything we were doing at that stage, then there's no way we would be able to deal with the later stages. Only the strong survive the process so it's the kindest thing to do.

Anya and I were separated. We both found it unusual having to dance with other people after so many years of dancing together, but we understood that was all part of the game. We'd feature in the show independently from now on, in any case – the rules prohibit competing as a double act. As of now, we would have to dance with various partners and within groups of dancers, all of us from different backgrounds and disciplines. Over and over again, we were given just a limited amount of time to learn a dance from one of the choreographers and perform it in front of the judges. Each time this happened, some of us would be eliminated.

On top of that, once at the end of the day we were asked to choreograph a routine in groups to present to the judges the next morning. We were all so tired, physically and emotionally, from pushing ourselves so hard that we couldn't think straight to devise new and exciting moves within our routines. This would create conflict within the group and separate the competitors who could cope with that kind of stress from those who couldn't. Of course, it also made for great TV.

I was used to pushing myself hard. Even as a child, I was

always intent on exceeding my limits when training. The tiredness we were all enduring and the relentlessness of the day-to-day training wasn't the thing that tested me most, though. What I found so difficult was the variety in the styles of dance we were learning and performing.

We were going to have to showcase a range of different dance styles over the course of the audition period and – if we made it through – during the live shows, so this was our chance to get them down pat. Over a period of just a few days, I was suddenly having to do hip hop, jazz and freestyle, having danced nothing but ballroom and Latin since the age of seven. It was like learning a new language, only harder because two languages can co-exist in your brain but taking on a new style of dance involves unlearning what you already know and erasing gestures that have become instinctual. I had to put all my years of ballroom training into a little box in the back of my head and store it away for when I next needed it.

Hip hop was the biggest challenge. Anya and I had only three or four hip hop classes in which to master the whole style and flavour of the genre. When I learn any new step, I do so by first grasping and then honing the technique. That's how I've been accustomed to learning dance for as long as I can remember. Ballroom and Latin are very precise in that sense. They are all about fine-tuning your balance and training your muscles to perform in a certain way; it cannot be rushed. You have to have the time and patience it takes to get each individual move down to a fine art. I was in a situation where I was going into hip-hop class and saying, 'Teach me the essence of this dance,' and my teacher was responding, 'It's more about attitude than technique.' It was completely alien to me.

I knew I was nowhere near as good as I wanted to be at the other dance styles but I just didn't think I could try harder, so I didn't know what I could do to make myself better. For a perfectionist like me, the situation was intolerable. I am my own worst critic even at the best of times so I was beating myself up constantly inside.

Ballroom dancing is just the same as my Russian accent. Even though I haven't lived in Russia for many years, it's still possible to tell I'm Russian when I speak and, no matter which language I'm speaking, I know I must always be speaking it with an inflection that conveys my roots. It's just the same with ballroom dancing. It's my default mode, so even if I'm dancing a completely different style, it's always my instinct to do so with the flavour and attitude of a ballroom dancer.

I'd asked my hip hop teacher, Beverley, to teach me the 'essence' of hip hop, thinking, if I could just understand that, then the rest of the moves would come easily. I was desperate to grasp the one thing that would mean I'd cracked the style. Now I understand that I was asking her the impossible. To learn the 'essence' of ballroom would take years, but, if shows like *Strictly Come Dancing* and *So You Think You Can Dance* prove anything, it's that it is possible to master a style to the extent you can showcase them in a way that is entertaining and appears reasonably competent from the outside, and that was exactly my task in this situation.

Beverley explained to me that hip hop was not formulaic. She asked me to create an image in my head, one in which I was angry at the world, and then to communicate that aggression through my movements. She told me that the way I moved my arms was too smooth and too 'pretty'. I'd spent decades training my arms to be that smooth and pretty yet, here I was, trying to unravel something hardwired into me.

People think that, if you're good at one type of dancing, then you must be able to turn yourself to any dance. That would be like going to China, speaking English and then wondering why no one could understand you because you are still, technically, speaking. Kimberley Walsh was in a similar situation, but reversed when I partnered her for *Strictly Come Dancing* in the 2012 series. Everyone knew she had danced with Girls Aloud and that she had rhythm, so there was this big expectation for her to be really good at ballroom from day one, even though it's a completely different discipline. Of course it helped in the beginning that she had the ability to move, but I was still teaching her a totally new skill.

In the end, the way I attempted hip hop was by trying different techniques to get myself into the mental place I needed to be to turn off everything I knew about dancing up until that point. I tried to meditate and imagine myself as a blank sheet of paper. Then I'd go to the gym and rehearse the moves in front of the mirror again and again until the routine resembled something like how I thought a hip hop dancer might move.

It was so hard for a ballroom boy!

I didn't know at that time that there would be a very big upside to all of this. In the same way as I have a Russian accent, certain phrases and words that I say sound very American because I have spent so many years in the States. I can liken my American speaking inflection to the way of learning other styles of dance in Las Vegas by putting different accents into my ballroom dancing. In retrospect, I can only see this as the great thing it was. It would take years and years of dancing nothing but hip hop to make me any worse at ballroom, but even now I can still drizzle a little of the hip hop I learned for *So You Think You Can Dance* into my ballroom routines to make them more exciting.

The great Fred Astaire was one of the first dancers ever to do this. He mixed tap and ballroom dancing. No one had ever seen a dancer merge together two distinct styles in that way before, so everyone got very excited. His work was considered extremely avant-garde at the time. Being different made Astaire popular and so other artists copied him, and now peppering one dance genre with another is so commonplace it's actually expected of you. These days, dance is all about flavour and 'mixing it up' – that's the direction in which the art form has evolved. *So You Think You Can Dance* primed me for that.

I know now that, once you reach a certain level within your skill, it's good to start experimenting. But at the time I'm describing, in Vegas, I was as far from my comfort zone as it was possible for me to be.

My hip hop audition was a low point. I was trying to remember what I'd been told by Beverley, back in New York. All I could recall was that she kept on telling me that I 'just had to feel it' and all I could think was: 'How?' Dancing hip hop in front of the judges, I did not perform anywhere near as well as I would have liked. They gave some negative feedback, but they could never have been as harsh on me as I was on myself in that moment. I didn't have the capacity to be kind to myself or to see what I was doing was like taking a fish out of water and asking it to fly.

I was convinced I hadn't made it through to the next rounds

in Los Angeles. With a sinking feeling, I flew back to New York, certain I had failed and that my brief foray into television was at its end.

Over the next few weeks, everyone who had taken part in the *So You Think You Can Dance* Las Vegas stages had nothing to do but wait. We waited while our criminal records, medical history and backgrounds were checked. We waited to hear from the producers about the logistics of what would happen next. But, most of all, we were waiting for the crucial judges' decision that would decide our fate.

Altogether, there were 40 dance acts to make it through to the training rounds in Vegas and of those only 20 of us would be selected for the show. We had a 50:50 chance of getting through and by that point I had lost the ability to know if my odds were any higher or lower than that: Vegas had knocked my confidence.

I compared my experience in Las Vegas to what happens when you put a lobster in boiling water. You are actually, in the kindest and most efficient way possible, preparing the creature for what comes next but it's so fast and so brutal in its nature. I had not expected the difficulties I'd encountered in trying to get to grips with hip hop and jazz, or not being able to make my body do the things that I imagined in my mind. It wasn't a problem I'd ever experienced in the past. My gut feeling was that I didn't think I'd done enough to get through and I can't deny feeling nervous about that.

What I *was* sure of was that now I *really* wanted the opportunity I'd once been uncertain about. I'd gone from not even being sure if it was the right thing to audition to deciding to commit myself fully to the process, to being desperate to see it through to its conclusion. Going to Las Vegas had changed my perspective. The competition was starting to mean something to me, and I'd never had my destiny so completely tied up in someone else's hands before. There was nothing more that I could proactively do to influence the situation – the whole situation was frustrating.

All 40 of us contestants were called back to CBS Studios in Los Angeles, where *So You Think You Can Dance* is shot, in May 2007. This part of the show was called 'The Green Mile', named after the walk prisoners on death row have to take from their cell to their fate. Naming it that added a sense of drama to proceedings. The judges had made their decision and we were there to receive the verdict. We were taken to a central holding area and, one by one, called in to a small room on the side to learn whether we would be staying in Los Angeles or we were being sent home.

I can still recall exactly how it felt to be sitting in that holding area at CBS Studios. Anya went in before me and discovered that she had made it through. The numbers sitting in the area slowly diminished as people went in to hear the decision made only to emerge from the judges' lair laughing or crying, depending on what they had been told. I'm not generally a person who tends to anticipate things, or even really evaluates them as they are happening; I'm fully present in whatever moment I'm experiencing and I don't think about the implications until later on, if at all. So it was strange for me when, sitting in the *So You Think You Can Dance* waiting area, I found myself thinking, My whole life has been building up to this moment. Usually, these are not sentiments that I would ever think or feel. As a rule, I don't tend to dramatise or hyperbolise events but I found myself being swept up in the energy of the room, the show and the past few weeks.

The atmosphere was so tense. It was as though all 40 of us were collectively holding our breath and it was being released, one-fortieth at a time, in a small wave of euphoria or crushing disappointment. I realised that, when you see people on reality TV shows talking about how 'it's all they've ever wanted' or 'this is the most important thing they've ever done', they're not faking it. You genuinely build yourself up to believing and saying those things. It feels like the most crucial and dramatic thing that will ever happen to you.

Seeing those who had been told they were leaving, I had mixed emotions. I knew for every person who came back with a negative verdict that increased my chances of getting through, but we had grown close during our time in Vegas and I felt sorry to see them go. Also, I felt a guilt that I couldn't properly explain. I knew how badly some of the contestants wanted to do the show and, even though I wanted it too, somehow knowing how they felt made me feel uncomfortable with how much I was hoping that I would be one of the successful 20. In taking a place in the live shows, it would mean another person who wanted it just as much as I did would have to go home.

By the time it was my turn to go into the judges' room, I had developed a fear. I feared not knowing what they were about to say but I also feared the possibility of their sending me home. I'd worked myself up into as emotional a state as it's possible for a boy from Siberia to get into, although I'm told I still appeared collected and calm on the outside.

Apart from ballroom, I knew that I hadn't done well when I

performed the dance styles during the auditions. I worried about that and it was even starting to make me doubt my ability as a ballroom dancer. Somehow, I'd managed to forget that I'd worked for almost 20 years, for 14 or 15 hours per day, to get to that point and I found myself thinking maybe the other dancers were better than me.

There are five or six different judges who tell you whether you have got through to the live shows, all sitting in a line as you stand opposite them on a dark stage. I remember Nigel Lythgoe and Mary Murphy (two of the main judges from the show) being there but by then I had worked myself up so much that the rest of the faces were a blur. Together, the judges told me that from their perspective I could have done better in Vegas. They said what I already knew: that I hadn't seemed comfortable dancing outside my own style. It sounded as if they were building up to something bad…

Then they told me that I'd made it through!

The people I know who watched my reaction to the judges' decision on screen tell me that I simply smiled and said thank you. Obviously, my Russian programming never lets me appear as elated as I am feeling on the inside. In reality, when I learned that I would be staying in Los Angeles and taking part in the live shows, I was light-headed with relief and excitement. Unlike when I was told that I was going to Vegas a few months earlier, I didn't even take a second to think about the next phase of the competition, or anything that had brought me to that point; I was totally enveloped in a feeling of exhilaration.

This was my 'victory moment'.

For that brief snatch of time, it was as though nothing else in the world existed. I realised that I'd been in a land of uncertainty for a long time. I'd taken a gamble and, when I did, it was as if I'd dived into water. Now, it felt as if I'd broken the surface and I was taking in huge gulps of fresh air.

I was just so happy to be alive.

Chapter 13

CITY OF
ANGELS

So You Think You Can Dance began filming in June 2007, so I had a few weeks off between hearing the judges' decision at the Green Mile and when the show began to tie up loose ends.

I returned to New York and shared my good news about having made it through the audition process with my friends, students and my mum back home. Always, I said the same thing: that I would be away for a few months to record a television show but I'd be back soon. I remember Margaret, the student with me in Puerto Rico when I got sick, saying to me, 'I just have this feeling that this is it, and that you won't be back, Pasha.' I told her that she should stop being silly, that I had a life in the Big Apple and, anyway, I wasn't particularly fond of Los Angeles.

How wrong I would turn out to be.

All 20 of the *So You Think You Can Dance* finalists were put up in the same apartment block in LA, with two of us sharing each apartment. We arrived a couple of days before the rehearsal process and filming began, giving us just enough time to settle into our new home and learn a little about the logistics of the journey we were about to embark on.

The first thing I remember after arriving at the apartment I was to share with another male dancer, Ricky, was the fridge. One of the people who worked on the show said to us, 'You have a fridge and we will fill it with whatever you want, just tell us what to get.' My list of foods was actually really short compared to what some of the other contestants said they needed. Some of them had been struggling financially, still trying to make it in the industry, so they hadn't been able to afford any luxury foodstuffs for a while. They were ordering all the different treats they loved but hadn't had the money to buy back in their hometowns. For me, it sort of summed up the magic of television, the idea that we'd go off to our rehearsals and come back to find the fridge magically filled with all the foods we had requested. I thought it was amazing.

In the same way, we went instantly from handling all the bits and pieces of our everyday lives to having everything mapped out and taken care of for us. We were no longer in control of our schedules; we didn't decide when we worked and when we didn't. It was a weird feeling, but at the same time there was a sweet sort of relief in it. All we had to do was wake up on time and then we were taken from place to place – rehearsals, costume fittings, press interviews, for which we didn't get any training – it all just happened so seamlessly and without us having to think about it.

Later, I reflected on how easily and quickly I had got used to that lifestyle. It was nice having nothing to worry about and nothing to focus on but the dance task at hand. I suppose I took it for granted a little bit at first.

So You Think You Can Dance has a format whereby in the initial stages, you dance in pairs but you are judged as individuals. For the first week of the show, the judges chose our dance partners, as well as the dances we would perform. I was paired with a girl named Jessi and we were told we would be dancing a waltz. That was a pretty easy first dance for me, although it was a little harder for Jessi, but that was where my background as a teacher came in useful. I'd been dancing the waltz for almost 20 years! Not having to frantically try to grasp a whole new style of dancing as I had in Vegas actually allowed me a little time to chill out and explore my temporary new home.

It was during this time that I saw a completely different side to Los Angeles. Of course, it wasn't the first time I had been there, but it was the first time I hadn't just been from the airport to the hotel and back again. On previous visits, the city had not impressed me but, during the course of *So You Think You Can Dance*, I began to completely fall in love with it.

LA is totally flat so the landscape and architecture is all laid out in front of you as far as the eye can see. Over to one side are the famous Hollywood Hills, which to me always look as though they are cuddling the main city. The hills always appear to me to be a benign presence – when you are in Los Angeles, it's as if they protect and watch over you.

You cannot see the stars in LA, which is ironic if you think about it, what with it having a reputation for being a place populated by some of the biggest film and music stars on the planet. Where the city is surrounded by hills, the smoke and exhaust fumes from all the cars have nowhere to go, so the sky always appears white or yellowish in hue. I have never once seen a piece of blue sky there but the yellow of the sky looks mellow more than menacing.

New York had been crammed with people and traffic; everything was in constant motion, moving super-fast. It's a financial capital and so everything was brisk and business-like. Los Angeles is far more relaxed in its energy. There are lots of wide avenues and highways that somehow appear to take on a kind of languid attitude because they are so stretched out.

The weather in LA in June wasn't hot and stuffy as Vegas had been in the previous months, rather a pleasant 25 degrees but the best thing about the climate was the breeze. The air moves in LA; it isn't stagnant as it had been in Vegas, so it felt really fresh. It gets a little chilly in the evening, so we'd have to plan our outfits for the day, taking a light sweater with us in the mornings so we didn't get cold and I enjoyed that, in a strange way.

New York City had felt as though it was buzzing. All the motion and energy was potent and concentrated, and that had been exciting to me when I first arrived from Moscow. I'd been swept up in the pure urgency of the place. What was interesting to me about LA was that it managed to be so laid-back yet it didn't lose any of the sense of anticipation or the feeling of possibility I'd found so attractive about New York. After all, Hollywood is where those who want to be stars come. There's no lack of ambition or drive, it just isn't as frantic as New York.

Everything seemed easy and I felt at peace. It's just so comfortable to be in Los Angeles in every sense, from the pace of life to the way the city is laid out and the weather. The whole spirit of the place makes you feel as if you're on vacation. But, of course, I was not holidaying, I was there to do some of the most challenging work of my career.

Chapter 14

AMERICA'S FAVOURITE DANCER

As it turned out, Ricky (with whom I was sharing a room) was the first contestant to leave *So You Think You Can Dance*.

I was surprised that he had been picked to go home so early. He was a great dancer, in my opinion. Although trained in contemporary and jazz, in the first week he had been chosen by the judges to do a tango. I thought that was kind of unfair because he wasn't a ballroom dancer and tango is a difficult dance to master when you have no experience of the style. I would say that tango is probably the hardest of all the classic Latin and ballroom routines. I could really relate to how Ricky must have been feeling, trying to get his body to tango. Dancing ballroom took him way out of his comfort zone, just as trying to dance hip hop had done for me.

I remember that I tried to help Ricky out because he was so

unlucky to have the tango as his first challenge. I felt bad for him, especially when you factor in that I had been given a waltz, which I'm pretty sure I could dance in my sleep! I'd tried to give Ricky some guidance and training in how to do the dance correctly and make it look really professional. Back at the apartment, I was helping him with little things like his posture and arm placement. By the time we had finished, I thought that he looked great but obviously the viewing public and the judging panel disagreed.

Ricky and I had got along really well. I think, if he had stayed longer, we would have become great friends. As it happened, though, I had the apartment to myself until such time as another male dancer left the competition and evened up the numbers again so we could share.

My waltz with Jessi was to be choreographed by Tony Meridith and Melanie La Patine from the studio in Times Square. This just goes to show what a small world the dancing industry is! You are always coming across the same faces. I was very happy to be working with Tony and Melanie again. My first week was full of things that were comfortable and familiar.

I didn't just have the waltz to contend with, though. Each week, we also had to dance a group number. We did the group routine as part of the results show, which was filmed the day after the main show.

In week one, our choreographer for the group number was Wade Robson. Within the dance community, Wade is completely iconic. He appeared in three of Michael Jackson's music videos for tracks on the *Dangerous* album in the mid-1990s. It's quite something for him to be able to say that, at 10 years old, he was dancing next to Michael Jackson. Then, in the late 1990s, he went on to choreograph music videos for artists like Britney Spears and *NSync, even though he was still really young. It's fair to say Wade is at the top of his game!

From the people that Wade has worked with, you can probably get a sense of the kind of dancing style he has. It's very unique and edgy, and you can tell it's been heavily influenced by the way that Michael Jackson moved.

Wade exposed me to a way of working that was completely new to me. In ballroom, the character of the dances and the story you are telling when you dance them is pretty much already set in stone before you start to choreograph. With the dance styles I was used to, the music we danced to might affect the rhythm of the routine but not the steps you make or the message that you are trying to convey with your movements. For example, the waltz will always be lyrical, soft, smooth and romantic. The tango always has a theme of jealousy running through it. Most Latin and ballroom dances are about the dynamic between a man and a woman; they make you think about love and all that goes with it. The exception is the paso doble, in which the male half of the partnership is supposed to be a matador (a Spanish bullfighter) and the female half is often perceived to be a bull, but in reality she is meant to be his cape. When dancing the paso, I simply see my partner as a feisty Spanish lady who is playing hard to get!

In ballroom competitions, we never knew what music we would be dancing to. Lots of couples took to the floor at the same time to dance the routines they'd been practising in their own studios. We were all dancing to the same song, so we'd try to mould the dance to fit the character of the music, adding accents to fit the theme of the song. When you have been dancing with someone for a long time, you don't need to stick rigidly to the routine you have rehearsed. You can just touch them on their arm or waist in a certain way and they will know what it is you want them to do, so you might wind up moving in a different direction to the one you have rehearsed.

The smart coaches would teach us the routines in measures. Depending on the dance, a 'measure' is three or four beats long and the measures group together usually in groups of eight. By breaking up the dance in this way, it meant that we could be more flexible and change the routines at the last minute so that they looked as though they were made to fit whatever song we were dancing to.

We would never pick a song because it represented an emotion or sentiment that we wanted to express within the dance and work from there. But that is the point from which Wade started on our first group number. With each dance, all of the *So You Think You Can Dance* choreographers were trying to convey a message. Straightforward ballroom doesn't translate to television in the same way as it does live. On camera, more than ever, dance has to tell an original story that the audience are not used to.

So, I was in a situation where I was learning a dance backwards.

Wade's choreography on week one was not that difficult for me. We each had our own segment where the camera was focused on us and the rest of the time we were just standing around so it wasn't too taxing. I guess he was easing us in during the first week. What was hard was trying to replicate exactly what he was doing. Being a dancer himself, as well as a choreographer, he dances his own routines in the most amazing way you have ever seen. For me, it was a revelation the first time I saw him move that anyone could dance like that. Afterwards, Wade became like a dance god in my eyes.

None of us contestants could even come close to what he was showing us but that didn't stop him from rehearsing us until we were as near to his performance style as we could possibly be. He wanted us to enact the moves in exactly the same way as he did because he was as close to perfection as it is possible to be.

When all 20 of us performed Wade's dance number during the live show, we were dressed in black and white mono-chrome, in a sixties kind of style. The fact that we were all dressed the same, combined with us trying to dance the same way as Wade had shown us, meant that it was really difficult to tell the various contestants apart. It totally made sense for the spirit of the dance, but it might have been confusing for the audience that we all looked the same in the week when they were first properly introduced to the finalists. Even now, I watch the footage of that performance back and I'll be straining to see which one is Anya – someone whose dancing I'd usually be able to recognise in an instant.

For the one- or two-eighths I was dancing with the camera on me, I was in a pack with the other male dancers. We were dancing a combination of hip hop, contemporary and jazz. The tone was kind of jaunty; it was a sort of mass-flirt between us male dancers and the girls, who were also dancing in a pack. It was supposed to be highly intense and dramatic. Those other dancers were more used to doing Wade's style of movement so I was totally focused on trying to keep up with them and doing my best to appear as comfortable and competent as they were.

I also had to look like I was enjoying myself and knew exactly what I was doing.

Later in the competition, all the other contestants and I performed a solo choreographed by Wade. For me, that was really challenging because again we were all trying to look the same and dance the solo the way Wade performed it. Afterwards, Nigel Lythgoe commented he would have liked to have seen more individuality in each of our performances.

Each week, the two people who would leave the competition were selected from the three couples with the lowest number of votes. On the first results show, one of the dancers who found themselves in the bottom six was Sabra Johnson, the girl who went on to win the entire competition and the $250,000 prize! It was the judges who would ultimately decide who went home and who got to stay for another week to try to prove they had more potential.

So, we all had this dual challenge. We had to show the judges that we were versatile and that we could deal with any dance they threw at us, but then we had to appear likeable on television, too. For a reserved kind of person like me, not prone to wearing his heart on his sleeve, it was hard to do what I had to do to convey my personality onto the screen.

For the first time, I wasn't just trying to be the best dancer I could possibly be technically. This time, I was aiming to be America's favourite dancer.

Chapter 15

JOINED-UP WRITING

Quite early on in the process of taking part in *So You Think You Can Dance*, I realised the key to becoming proficient isn't just about the steps. You can do each step with skill but the dance will never look good unless you learn how to join them up. What you do between each movement is just as important as the movement itself and often shapes the way that the routine is received.

The attitude of a dance is all about the space between the moves.

The only thing that I can really liken this to is learning how to do joined-up writing. Once you are able to write letters joined together, the entire act of writing becomes so much easier and faster, less time consuming. Joined-up writing generally requires less thought, it's automatic; it also looks like your writing, as it's individual and unique to you. You're putting your own stamp on the pre-designed letters.

Joined-up writing takes time, though. You have to have been writing for a little while before you can do it. It's exactly the same in learning a new style of dance. You can learn and perfect each individual move but it takes a certain amount of time to instinctually know what you should do, going from one move to another.

I was able to go through this process mentally and physically while ballroom dancing as a matter of course; I didn't even have to put any thought into it. I'd got so used to telling myself a story over and over in my head that it guided me through the process between steps so that it was now completely instinctual.

The experienced hip hop dancers on *So You Think You Can Dance* were in the same way automatically programmed to make the dance look like hip hop should. There are a lot of staccato types of movement within hip hop but if they are enacted in that way, without the joining factor, then it looks awkward. Just like if you were to write each letter of a sentence individually without joining them up – even though you are still writing and what you are writing can be understood, it would look awkward, clumsy and a little wrong. So that was why it became more important than ever for me to rehearse the *So You Think You Can Dance* contemporary and hip hop routines in front of a mirror until they appeared fluid and effortless. It was the only method I had found that seemed to be effective in honing me into the rounded dancer I was trying to be. For me, there was no logic in which dance moves followed one another so I had to create logic purely through something visual I could lock into my memory.

Over and over, I would return to my apartment after rehearsals so tired that I could barely stand and force myself to practise the routine all over again in front of my bathroom mirror. It took a lot of endurance but I couldn't think of another way to do what I had to do in the time period.

Ricky going home from the competition had given us all a shock and impressed upon us how hard we were going to have to work, if we wanted to stay. Of course we knew that two people had to leave each week and those were the rules of the game we were playing, but that didn't make it any easier to lose someone you'd grown close to. That feeling of loss is something I continue to observe in every television show I have made so far. Because of the nature of these dance shows, you're working so intensely with people and you get close to them so when they have to go back home, as they always do eventually, it can be a blow. Even now when I perform in *Strictly Come Dancing*, I feel a little sad when any of the celebrity contestants leaves the show because you get to feel like a temporary family.

The only thing that you can do to try to deal with the constant state of change when you're filming is to focus completely on the next task you have to accomplish. That's how I made it from week to week on *So You Think You Can Dance*. I didn't take the time to look around me or compute what was going on, I just thought about my next dance and how I was going to get it right.

In week one, it had been in the judges' hands what dance we would be performing. From week two onwards, we pulled the names of the dances out of a hat so they were selected at random, although you wouldn't be able to dance the same style as you had the week before. While I was dancing with Jessi, she would always tell me what she was hoping we would get that week and somehow I had this knack of being able to pull that dance out of the hat. I didn't ever really hope for one dance over another, but she had a very clear idea of what she wanted us to do. So she'd wish it and I'd make it happen. I'm still not sure how I did that.

Looking back, I think the judges decided to put Jessi and me together for two reasons. The first is that our physiques matched. We are both quite slight and not particularly tall so we looked good together. The second reason is that our personalities were complete opposites. She is very bubbly, always giggling and screaming, and creating a certain amount of drama. I am very calm. So I think maybe the producers saw that we would balance each other well.

Jessi and I had great comments about our waltz in week one. For example, Dan Karaty said that usually our style of dance 'bored' him but that it was a 'pleasure' to watch us because we seemed like we were 'floating around the floor'. Training had all worked out really well because, even though she wasn't trained in ballroom, Jessi was a great dancer, which gave her a foundation, and I had a lot of experience in teaching people ballroom technique. It was easy for me to teach Jessi waltz after teaching ballroom and Latin to amateurs who didn't have her flexibility or general background. For me, the most important thing was to make sure that she felt comfortable doing the routine and I think I succeeded in doing that.

I now know that afterwards Jessi said on camera, 'Every girl dreams of dancing a beautiful dance like the waltz with a guy like Pasha.' I didn't see when she filmed that part at the time, otherwise it might have hinted at what was to happen later. Back then, I couldn't possibly have known what the future had in store and I was just happy to have made it through to the second round.

Jessi and I had picked out a jazz routine. The choreographer we were assigned was Tyce Diorio. Tyce's calibre is just as impressive as Wade's. He has worked choreographing dances for Jennifer Lopez, Janet Jackson and Paula Abdul. Also, he won an Emmy for outstanding choreography in 2009.

Again, Tyce was an incredible dancer himself, in addition to being a choreographer, and I was destined to learn a lot from him. The best piece of advice he ever gave me was when he was talking about auditions. I can't remember the exact words he used but they were something along the lines of: 'Even if you are dancing in the back row, 20 rows back, you have to project out and make sure that the audience don't see anyone but you.' He emphasised to us the fact that, when it comes to auditions, you only get that one shot and there are no excuses for letting the opportunity slide. You can't say that you were having a bad day, or were in the wrong place on the stage; it's up to you to do everything you can to grab that chance.

The other favourite piece of advice I was given during *So You Think You Can Dance* was from Mia Michaels, another of the choreographers on the show. She told us, 'Don't be a needy dancer – just make it work.' That sums up a lot for me because so often it's your first instinct to try to find an excuse to get out of the things you find challenging or you don't think you will be able to do well. Whenever I have that instinct, I remember Mia's words.

Tyce came up with the most amazing jazz routine for Jessi and me to perform. I was so into it. The two of us would represent a pair of birds doing a kind of crazy mating ritual. In my mind, we *were* exotic birds, maybe from Africa.

The difficulty I had was that we had to dance the jazz routine barefoot. I had never, ever danced barefoot before. When you train as a ballroom dancer, from the very first time you dance, you have to wedge your feet into those tight little ballroom dance shoes. At first it's really uncomfortable but after a while they start to feel like a second skin and you can't imagine dancing without them. So when I was dancing barefoot it was giving me these huge blood blisters on my feet. They were *so* painful. I guess the other contestants had the same issue with wearing ballroom shoes because they were used to dancing barefoot.

Despite all that, I knew I had to work through the pain and, as Mia said, make it work. When it came down to it, I was so focused on getting my body to move in the way that Tyce wanted it to that I stopped noticing how much discomfort my feet were giving me.

Tyce is my kind of dance coach. He's coming from a place of fun and creativity but that doesn't stop him from being very, very demanding. He may be the most demanding person I have ever worked with.

During week two, Jessi was very tired and dehydrated. Tyce would always ask if she was okay and she'd complain that she was not. He'd sympathise for maybe half a second, he'd say, 'Oh you poor thing,' but then just plough on anyway and say, 'Right, let's do it one more time!' I think being that way was the dual sides of Tyce coming out. The dancer in him empathised with the exhaustion that we were feeling, while the choreographer in him was going to rehearse this routine until it was as perfect as it could be!

I was also getting really, really tired, but I thought to myself, I'll rest later. I knew that I only had a limited amount of time with this outstanding choreographer, who was imparting his wisdom. The task at hand was to 'fake it 'til I make it' and to seem as though I knew exactly what I was doing.

Finally, I was starting to dance in joined-up writing.

I was smart enough to know that my Russian ways and calm demeanour almost certainly wouldn't endear me to the American public. Usually, American reality television is all about wearing your heart on your sleeve and keeping emotions close to the surface. People in the US are used to their TV stars screaming and crying, and talking candidly about how they feel. Such behaviours definitely didn't come naturally to me but, until I was able to better show that I was a human being, not a dancing cyborg, I was never going to be thought of as a contender for 'America's favourite dancer'.

I had proof of this when, in week two, Jessi and I found that we were one of the three couples who had received the least votes from the viewing public. We were so disappointed.

In the run-up to our performance, I'd been practising our exotic bird jazz routine a lot on my own. Jessi didn't seem herself. I'd got to know a very energetic and bubbly character in Vegas and during the first week of the competition, but now she just seemed really tired all the time. When rehearsing our waltz in week one, I had so many things to say to Jessi to help her get the dance right, but in week two she had only given me a couple of tips on how to dance jazz, even though that was her area of speciality. With each day that passed, she was becoming quieter, moodier and more withdrawn.

Jessi had shared with me that she had a few issues with her body image at that time. She was a very skinny girl anyway and yet she was always doing something to try to make herself even slimmer than before. I wondered whether that was preying on her mind. Also, I suspected she wasn't taking proper care of herself, drinking enough water or eating enough. In spite of all that, I had thought we danced our jazz routine well, so it was a little upsetting to find ourselves faced with the prospect of elimination.

Even worse than the feeling of disappointment at not getting the votes we needed was the knowledge that I'd have to dance a solo routine during the results show to fight for my right to stay. The idea filled me with horror. Until then, the only dancing I had ever done had been either with a partner or as part of a group. A big part of how I danced was in reacting and feeding off the performance of the other people or person on stage. I just wasn't sure how I was going to handle it out there on my own.

Each week, every contestant has to prepare a different 30-second solo routine in case they find themselves in one of the bottom three couples. We choreographed it ourselves but sometimes sought advice from the other contestants to try to improve it. I'd rehearsed my routine, all the while hoping I'd never actually have to perform it.

If you are the male dancer, the whole craft of ballroom dancing is about showing off your partner. I had always seen myself as being like a frame and my female partner was the picture within that frame. She would bring all the colour and movement to draw your eye in, and I was keeping her where she needed to be. My role within the ballroom dance is very important but it's subtle and characterised by not drawing too much attention to myself. It's just the same now when I dance with Katya during our live touring show, which is called *An evening with Katya and Pasha*. I always see it as being more about her than it is about me. The way I view things, if I make Katya look good, then it makes us look good as a team and everyone wins. That's the sort of dancing dynamic I am used to. The upshot of having been in a ballroom state of mind for so long was that I didn't know how to shine on my own.

After we devised our solo routines, we'd show them to Jeff Thacker. He'd give us comments on how we could make them better. For example, he'd say things like, 'You need to wow the audience straight away. You can't spend 20 seconds warming up and getting into the routine because you only have 30 altogether.'

I always really appreciated what Jeff had to say. Despite Jeff seeming a little intimidating at first, I quickly learned he had our best interests at heart. Again, he had been a dancer himself so that put him in a good position – he could see things from our perspective as contestants, as well as from that of a producer trying to make good television.

Jeff also has an elephantine ability never to forget anything. He can tell you what he ate for dinner 20 years ago, at which restaurant and on what street. Everything is recalled down to the smallest detail, which is another reason why he is so good at his job.

I liked that Jeff and I were able to have a little banter. Over the course of the show, I grew fond of him and now I would count him as one of my friends.

But back to my daunting first solo results show performance. I chose to dance a jive because I thought it might calm my nerves. When you perform a jive with a partner, there are many times when you dance the same steps side-by-side without touching. I was hoping that I'd be able to perform the jive solo and it would feel sort of similar. I thought of it as a way of bridging the gap between my comfort zone and what I had to do.

All those efforts didn't stop me from absolutely hating my first solo performance, though. When I watched the routine back, I could see it wasn't my best ever jive but that's because I couldn't get over the feeling that there should have been someone next to me, as I was used to. Fortunately, the judges saw potential and chose to keep me safe to dance another week in the competition.

I learned from the experience of doing the jive solo that I would have to find a way to create the sense of a partner, even if I happened to be dancing alone. If I got to the more advanced stages of *So You Think You Can Dance*, I knew that I would have to dance solo, whether or not I was in the bottom three couples. It was a requirement and there was no getting around it. So I devised a solo routine that mixed a few different dances together (including Viennese waltz and samba), where there was a mannequin in a ballroom gown on stage, and another solo paso doble where I used a cape. Having these props was instantly comforting, I found.

After knowing what it was like to be in the bottom three, the experience of being in the show became so much more intense. From then on, you always have it in your thoughts that there was a time when the audience watching at home didn't think you were good enough and it preys on your mind.

I still find the experience of being in the bottom two

couples on the results shows on *Strictly Come Dancing* stressful, even to this day. Those few seconds when you're standing there waiting for the judges to deliver their decision are so tense that afterwards you always feel like a squeezed lemon. Even if you are saved and make it through to the next round, you are left wondering why the public didn't relate to your routine when you thought it was great. There's also the impact of seeing the other couple drop out and watching them when they sometimes cry as their journey comes to an end. It's always so emotional.

My first experience of 'dancing for my life' on *So You Think You Can Dance* left me feeling like a string on a violin that had been pulled so tight it was almost ready to snap. I was left feeling vulnerable and deflated.

I was so desperate for the experience of being in *So You Think You Can Dance* not to come to an end. But it wasn't really about winning the whole show and it certainly wasn't about proving myself to be a better dancer than the other contestants; it was more about being able to remain in an environment with these wonderful, world-class choreographers and having the chance of another week to learn and expand my skill set.

I was training in new and exciting dance styles and having my horizons truly broadened; also living a life where all I had to think about was dancing. There was nothing else at all to concern me. It was a fantasy turned into reality, and I was determined to cling onto it with everything that I had.

Right then, I wasn't sure how I was going to cling, though. We were advised not to read any of the blogs or press about the show, so I could only guess how the American public felt about me, but instinct told me I needed to show more of my character. I couldn't figure out a way to reveal to America the real Pasha but still be myself. And then, life provided me with an opportunity to do just that.

Chapter 16

UNREQUITED LOVE

Four hours before we were due to dance our third live routine on *So You Think You Can Dance*, Jessi collapsed in the rehearsal studio and had to be taken into hospital.

During that third week, we had pulled the cha-cha-cha at random out of the hat and, once again, Tony and Melanie from my New York studio were to be our choreographers. It had looked set to be a really promising week for me. I got to dance a Latin dance, which I love to do and actually was my speciality, and we were working alongside people I knew, trusted and really liked.

Even in spite of those things, though, our schedule remained completely relentless. If we were to survive the demands we were making on our bodies, then we had to treat them well. We had to make sure that we were taking care of ourselves, eating enough of the right foods and drinking enough water to be able to handle the demands of our training timetable. It seemed to me as though Jessi wasn't doing any of those things.

Sure enough, in hospital she was diagnosed with dehydration and placed on a drip to get her well again. The doctors also advised that she should not dance that week.

Of course, I went with Jessi to the hospital to make sure that she was okay. I was very concerned about her health and stability, both physically and emotionally. To me, it seemed as if she was cracking under the pressure.

The cameras followed us to the hospital because they had to put together a quick video to play during the show, explaining why Jessi wouldn't be performing that week. They recorded a little interview with me as part of that video and I was wound so tight with the shock of Jessi collapsing so suddenly and the drama of the situation that I appeared to be on the verge of tears. Looking back, I don't remember feeling tearful. As far as I was concerned, I was just feeling a normal amount of worry as I would for anyone who was unwell, but being in the show obviously magnified the emotions I was experiencing.

I can see now, watching the footage of me at the hospital doing that interview and sitting by Jessi's bedside, how it might have seemed as if I had romantic feelings for her. There I was, almost crying in a hallway with real concern for this girl. It's easy to see why viewers would have jumped to that conclusion.

Completely by accident, I got the opportunity to show the viewing audience at home my sensitive side. *So You Think You Can Dance* fans responded with sympathy to my sad little face and the love story they believed was unfolding between Jessi and me; they took me into their hearts. After that, I was never in one of the bottom three again.

On the day that she collapsed, Jessi was given one live show off to recover and we were told that we could perform the routine during the results show later on. But I was well enough and the show's producers didn't let me off so lightly. I still had to find a way to dance the routine Jessi and I had been working on and show the audience what I had been doing all week in order to stay in the competition. In the end, they asked me to do my cha-cha-cha with Melanie, my choreographer.

Melanie really freaked out about this. She was the only female dancer who knew the steps so she couldn't get out of doing it and it was by this point only a couple of hours before we were going to be live on air, so she didn't have time to teach the routine to anyone else. But Melanie was not at all up for appearing on television.

Being a little older than she had been at the peak of her career, Melanie was worried that she wasn't in the best shape. She is still a fantastic dancer and I think that she looks great, but I guess she was comparing herself to how she used to look at the height of her fitness and abilities. The *So You Think You Can Dance* team found her a Latin-style dress to wear, which was of course a little skimpy because that's always the style. She felt so uncomfortable having to show off her body to an audience of millions that she ended up putting a big sweater over the top of it!

When I think about that cha-cha-cha I danced with Melanie and all the circumstances that brought it about, I think it's quite funny. It really did sum up that mentality of 'the show must go on', the way they pushed Melanie onto the stage at the last minute in a dress she didn't want to wear and there she was, in her big sweater.

Following the results show, the judges made the decision to let Jessi go. I guess they were worried about her and anticipated she might have to go into hospital again.

After she was told that she would be leaving the contest, Jessi was invited to say a few words. In her farewell speech, she declared to the whole of America that she was in love with me and wanted me to be her boyfriend. I was standing right beside her, hearing this news for the first time in front of an audience of millions.

At first, I wasn't at all sure why she said it. I wondered if it was perhaps a publicity stunt so that people would remember her for longer after she went out of the competition or she would get a few headlines out of it. Jessi was a very good-looking girl but I didn't have any romantic interest in her at all. The feelings she had for me were not reciprocated in any way and, as far as I was concerned, I had not given her any reason to think they would be.

Then I realised that Jessi must have mistaken the intention behind some of my actions. When you dance ballroom, you hold your partner very close, in a special way. You have to be strong and manly, and make her feel delicate and feminine in order to be able to perform ballroom routines in the way they are supposed to be danced. Jessi was used to dancing solo so no one had ever held her like that before. She had taken the chemistry we created through our dancing to mean something that it had not. Throughout my career, I have seen that this happens quite a lot, with people who don't know so much about ballroom dancing falling in love with their teachers because they misread the situation.

I think Jessi must have also misinterpreted me visiting her

in the hospital as confirmation that I felt the same way as she did.

When contestants were told they would be leaving *So You Think You Can Dance*, they pretty much went home straight away. They were given time to go back to their apartment, pack and say goodbye to everyone and then the show's co-ordinators would book them on a flight home, usually the very next morning. Normally, it felt a bit abrupt, people being taken away from the group so suddenly, but I found that it was a fortunate thing in Jessi's case. I didn't know what I was going to say to her if ever we were face-to-face alone.

After the incident of the 'live love declaration', I avoided speaking or spending any time with Jessi because I didn't want anything I did to be misinterpreted again and for her to build up any more of an idea of us becoming involved as boyfriend and girlfriend. If you don't know you are giving someone the wrong signals, it's one thing but, once you know you have, I always think it's cruel to spend any more time with that person because anything you say or do can give them false hope.

And then Jessi was gone.

After that, I was partnered with another girl named Sara. Sara was a really cool person and her specialist area was hip hop. We danced together well and by that point all the contestants were much more familiar with the process and what we needed to do to make it work. I remember that Sara and I had a lot of fun during rehearsals. The incident with Jessi and the hospital was enough for the American viewers to start seeing me as a human being with real feelings, and that was a good thing for my chances in the competition. In their eyes, I was now a three-dimensional personality.

I hadn't needed to shout or scream, or do anything out of character. Without really intending to do so, I had managed to put myself in the running, with a real chance of winning the entire show.

Chapter 17

WEST COAST SWING

My first dance with Sara remains to this day one of my most favourite routines that I have ever performed. She and I were working that week with a guy called Benji Schwimmer. The previous year, Benji had actually won season two of *So You Think You Can Dance* and had returned to do some of the choreography for the new season. He was famous for his brilliant West Coast Swing, one of the dances he had trained in from an early age. Happily, it was the dance that Sara and I had pulled out of the hat.

Whenever people talk about my performances on *So You Think You Can Dance*, it is always Benji's routine that they remember most clearly. I think it was partly down to Benji's talent, but also due to the fact that I was undergoing a transition as a dancer. I was starting to learn how to venture into uncomfortable territory and make myself the centre of attention.

It was around week three that Anya took me to one side and said she needed to talk to me about something important. Coming from a background of teaching ballroom and Latin to amateurs, she understood that I had actually trained myself not to fulfil my potential on stage. It makes sense when you think about it. As a teacher of ballroom, it was actually my job not to out-dance and overshadow my partner. It wasn't simply that I was trying to make my students look good, as I do with my professional partners, with my students I would deliberately not dance to the best of my ability so that I didn't make them look bad.

Without really thinking about it, I'd taken this tendency into performing with my partners on *So You Think You Can Dance*. They weren't amateurs of course, but also they weren't trained in ballroom and Latin in the same way as me so they were never going to be at the same standard. Instinctually, I was bringing myself down to their level.

Anya said, 'If you want to do well, you are going to have to start being more selfish.' She told me it was time I began thinking about me instead of always putting others first because, if I didn't, I would get lost in the background and I would have to say goodbye to this chance.

There was a kind of freedom in the realisation I had at that point; that I wasn't restricted by any form of obligation to my partner. All of us contestants were there for the same reason: to dance the very best we could. It wasn't a form of betrayal or doing my partner a disservice to try to shine because that's exactly what they were trying to do. For the first time in ages, I was at liberty to just let rip and dance in a way that had a chance of drawing eyes in my direction.

After that, I found that I started to think differently. I'm a person who constantly questions himself and his abilities. For that reason, I know exactly what my strengths and weaknesses are within my craft. Before *So You Think You Can Dance*, I always used to focus only on the negatives and try to identify where there was scope for improvement. After Anya's pep talk, I was able to see there are things that I can do better than other people can. I still want to continue to get better at dancing every day I'm alive, but I no longer see the sense in dwelling on the things I've found to criticise and being overly tough on myself. I know, for example, that one of the areas where I excel is in storytelling through my dance. I'm able to evoke all kinds of emotions, thoughts and memories in my audience and I need to play to that strength.

Watching video footage of the West Coast Swing I danced with Sara, I can see the changes in my performance style and in myself. I was projecting out more, making my movements more exaggerated and having more fun with the routine. It really marked a turning point for me.

Shortly after she gave me that key piece of advice, it was Anya's turn to leave the competition. She went home on 19 July 2007, having not made it to the top 10 finalists. I believe that she was incredibly shocked by her departure. She had not expected to go home at that stage. It came as an unwelcome surprise to me, too. When the camera caught a shot of my face as the judges announced that Anya would be the next dancer to make her exit, you can see that I had a few tears on my face.

The way that the filming of *So You Think You Can Dance* worked meant that we contestants were always able to watch the show back together as a group. The show aired at 8pm in all the different time zones in the United States. We would film at 5pm in LA so that it could transmit live at 8pm in New York. The show was two hours long in total, so we had time to go and get changed and do any final bits of filming before all heading over to one of our apartments to watch what we'd just filmed, 8pm Los Angeles time.

The results show was a little different. That was actually filmed the day after the first show of the same week, but was not screened until two days afterwards. The live audience were taken out of the studio before the result was announced so that they couldn't go on any of the social networking sites and reveal the outcome before it was broadcast on television.

So, after the results show, rather than heading back to the apartment block, we'd always go to The Grove. *So You Think You Can Dance* is filmed at CBS Studios on the crossing between Fairfax Avenue and Beverly Boulevard, which is also where they make *Dancing With the Stars* and *America's Got Talent*. The studio is situated next to a big shopping complex with shops and restaurants and that is what The Grove was. We'd all go there to have a meal and celebrate another week of being in the competition. Sometimes the person who was leaving the contest would come and join us and make it their farewell dinner, and sometimes not.

Anya did not come to The Grove. She literally went back to her apartment, packed and returned to New York. She didn't speak to me for the next few weeks. The next time we spoke was when all 20 of the original finalists were reunited for the last show of the series.

I think that Anya needed those couple of weeks to recover from what she maybe saw as an injustice between us. We never talked about it but I guessed the way that she saw things, it was she who had persuaded me to audition for *So You Think You Can Dance* and she had wanted it more than I had in the beginning. So for me to still be in the competition and getting something that she wanted meant that in her eyes I did not deserve it. It was her dream, and now I was the one who was getting to live it.

I'm only guessing at the way Anya felt and the reasons why she didn't call me during those few weeks. I tried to call her a couple of times but she did not pick up. It could have been for a different reason altogether. She was okay with me once we saw each other again when she returned for the final show. Yet, knowing Anya as well as I did, I suspect she resented my success at that stage.

At the point at which it all happened, I just didn't have the time or space in my head to think about whether the situation between Anya and me was fair or not. I have since thought about it, however, and I have concluded that, in fact, it was not unfair and I did deserve to still be in the running for *So You Think You Can Dance*.

In our culture, we all tend to have this idea that if you have something it has to be because it was your idea to begin with and you worked from nothing to get it. I perceive things slightly differently. As I have already said, I believe that, if you need something, life will find a way to provide it for you. Part of having that belief system is acknowledging that sometimes things come into your life because of someone else. That person is the implement life is using to give you the thing that you needed.

For example, say a friend of mine needs to get his car fixed but he doesn't have the money to do it. If I, as his friend, am able to pay for him to do so, then surely life is giving him what he needs in using me as a tool in order for him to receive it. It doesn't mean that he does not deserve to get it in the first place.

In just the same way, I couldn't have known it when we were back in New York, but I firmly believe that life was always taking me towards *So You Think You Can Dance*. Yes, it was Anya who pushed me into taking that opportunity and Jeff who persisted with the idea that I should join the show, but now I was there and able to realise the value of it, I wanted so much to hold onto what life had thrown my way.

Chapter 18

THE OTHER SIDE
OF THE COIN

It was the week of the semi-finals of *So You Think You Can Dance* and by that stage we were picking our dance partners, as well as our dances, out of a hat each week.

That week, I picked Lacey Schwimmer, who was the sister of Benji, the previous year's winner. Just like Benji, Lacey was a phenomenal dancer. She was mainly trained in West Coast Swing and jazz, but also a good all-rounder with the ability to apply herself to lots of different styles.

By this stage in the contest, there were only six contestants left and we had to dance two dances every week. For our first, Lacey and I devised a cheeky but complicated routine that told the story of a man who falls in love with a shop mannequin and takes it home. In the story, the mannequin comes to life to dance with the man.

It was really tough for Lacey to work out the mannerisms to

be able to convey that she was a mannequin. Imagine being a person having to play a plastic dummy who is magically turned into a person. It's a little like when Gwyneth Paltrow won the Oscar for *Shakespeare In Love* after she played a woman pretending to be a man, playing a woman! It must have been really confusing. Lacey worked really hard to get the dance technically correct, while still getting across the fun and playful nature of the routine. In the end, she did a fantastic job. A lot of the performance hinged on her facial expressions, as well as what she was doing with her body.

I still don't know whether I was supposed to be just some random pervert who stopped by the shop window and started to imagine that the mannequin was alive so he could fall in love with it, or whether the dummy really was magic in that story. Either way, I think it works.

After that routine, Lacey and I performed a beautiful, slow waltz. I was very proud of both dances. Lacey made it through to another week and got to perform in the final, but this time it was my turn to be sent home.

If I'm honest, leaving the competition that week came as a total shock to me. I had only been in the bottom three once during the course of the whole show. That had happened the week before Jessi got sick and it seemed such a long time ago. Week after week, I had been riding high, getting through to the next round. Based on that track record, I didn't see any reason why I wouldn't be dancing in the final. I fully expected to be there. Luckily, it was a quiet expectation. I had not been consciously pinning all my hopes on it.

When the news was announced that this time it would be me leaving *So You Think You Can Dance*, I felt an odd mixture of disappointment and relief. By then, it was week nine of the competition. We had been dancing non-stop for so long, with such a relentless schedule. It wasn't just the long hours of training – after all, I had known what it was like to train hard before I went to Vegas – it was the combination of that and having so many new routines to learn, along with the emotional pressure of it all. I was so exhausted in every way that it's possible for a person to be exhausted.

I knew that the contestants who made it through to the final would have to learn not two but four routines for the last show. There was a big part of me that thought, I'm so pleased I don't have to do that. That part of me was comforted by the prospect of having a rest. Another part of me knew that I would have found the strength and energy to dance the last week from somewhere. That was the part that frustrated me; my journey had come to an end just before the finish line.

All 20 of the finalists danced a group routine during the last show and so that meant we were in the CBS studio when the top four were practising their four dances. I remember looking at Sabra, Danny, Neil and Lacey, who were the four who had made it through to the final, and thinking they looked like ghosts. They were so exhausted and washed out, and now they had to pull the best performance of their lives out of the bag. I felt sorry for them on the one hand, but on the other I wanted to know what it would be like to experience that final frontier of fatigue. I'm a person who craves challenge and to dance four brand-new routines in the last show would have been my biggest dancing challenge to date.

The *So You Think You Can Dance* choreographers cleverly allowed us to put the stamp of our own personalities on each dance we performed and this became more and more pronounced the further we advanced through the contest stages. I would have liked to know what the dances I would have done in the final would have looked like. Between the dances, I think they would have summed me up as an artist. They would have said 'this is Pasha, in dance form'. I'm exceedingly sorry that I never got to the stage where that happened.

In the end, though, the last week of filming was a very happy and contented one for me. The disappointment I felt at not having made it through was only fleeting. I knew that I had worked the hardest I could, given the best I could give and ultimately done all that I could do. The only reason ever to regret something is when you know that you could have done better, but in this instance I couldn't see that I would have done anything differently, so I was pretty chilled. Ultimately, our fate lay in the hands of the voting public. For whatever reason, they hadn't voted for me but I was pleased to have got this far.

So You Think You Can Dance had changed my perspective on the kind of performer I wanted to be. During my time on the show, I had felt like a sponge, just soaking up the advice and expertise of all the influential people around me. I realised that I wanted to 'mix it up', just like some of the best dancers of our era. It was a way that I could make ballroom more modern and accessible for the masses.

In a way, when you incorporate new moves into familiar routines, you are building a bridge between the old and the new. You are taking a classic dance that everyone has seen before but adding a twist that makes it unique, fresh and exciting. In this way, your audience finds it easy to digest, not too strange and avant-garde, but you are still giving them something new. This was the way forward, I decided.

Learning hip hop, jazz and contemporary, it was as though my life was a coin and suddenly that coin had flipped over to reveal the other side after only ever seeing one side for so long. Ballroom and Latin represented one side of the coin but on the other were all these different ways of moving. I now had a whole spectrum to incorporate into the way I danced, previously not accessible to me.

It dawned on me that I was a million miles away from the person I had been when I first had to be persuaded to do the audition for *So You Think You Can Dance*. So much had happened to re-mould my view of the world. I'd been exposed to a whole new way of thinking and the upshot of it all was that I had fallen in love with dance again.

Doing my first television show made me realise that it wasn't just ballroom dancing that I adored. I loved to perform, regardless of the style of dance. Once again, I was excited by my art form. It was almost as if I remembered the reasons why dancing had been so attractive to me in the first place as a little boy, back in Siberia. Somewhere along the line between Siberia and New York, I'd managed to take the fundamental joy out of dancing. I'd been so focused on honing my craft that I was fixating on the things I didn't think I was good at and who was better or worse than me. I'd turned dance into something so technical it had stopped being about expression and creativity.

So You Think You Can Dance is a show that's all about connecting with your audience and making them feel certain things. I had realised that I was good at that. It wasn't just that I could do it – it was that I *loved* doing it. After years and years of competitions that took place purely in front of a panel of judges and dancing behind the closed doors of studios, I had discovered just how happy it made me to dance in front of an audience.

Even today, I still enjoy teaching other people to dance – after all, that's a huge part of my role on *Strictly Come Dancing*. I now know that has to be balanced with being able to perform myself and indulge that part of me, though.

Dancing had become like meditation again after taking part in *So You Think You Can Dance*. I was able to let go and feel with my body to try to create something magical. I could gauge and respond to the energy of the audience. It all gave me a huge rush of adrenaline and pleasure. Now I knew with absolute certainty that my future lay in dancing for an audience. Margaret had been right, I couldn't go back to the lifestyle I had created in New York City.

I was staying in LA.

Chapter 19

FALLING IN
LOVE AGAIN

A big part of the appeal of dancing on television is that it gives you the opportunity to be an ambassador for ballroom dancing and to make it popular with the masses.

Strictly Come Dancing has been responsible for a huge surge of people in Britain taking up ballroom classes since the show first aired in 2004. I'm so pleased about that because ballroom dancing is part of the historical culture of the country, as well as in America. If you talk to older people who were around during the 1940s, 50s or 60s, they all knew how to ballroom dance just as a social thing. They'd go to dances on the weekends in the same way that people go out clubbing now, but instead of just dancing randomly there'd be a band playing waltzes, foxtrots and quicksteps and they all knew the steps to each one.

Now, when I perform with Katya in our tour around

Britain and Ireland, we are always so moved to see the way that older couples in the audience often respond to our dances. Every performance, we will usually catch a glimpse of a couple with tears in their eyes or they'll give each other a special look, which lets you know that this particular dance is memorable to them. Afterwards, when we are signing programmes and meeting audience members, they will sometimes come up to us and say, 'We met while dancing a foxtrot,' or whatever it was. It's such a pleasure to be able to evoke that memory for them.

For me, ballroom and Latin dancing is a return to values that society is in danger of losing. You never hear older gentlemen say that they thought learning to dance was 'girly' – it was simply what they did and part of the mating ritual. Now, when you go into a dance school for young people, you'll invariably see only one or two young men there, which is a shame. Today, dancing is predominantly viewed as sport for girls.

In reality, dancing is one of the most genuinely manly things you can do. You have to be strong enough to lift your partner; you must guide and lead her through the dance. At the same time, you also have to be sensitive and caring towards her. The dances are all about love and showing in your performance that you are capable of love, so in the course of one dance you must be both soft and strong in order to get the balance right.

For me, real masculinity is about making a girl feel comfortable and look beautiful on the dance floor. You must be comfortable enough to let your partner express herself and for all eyes to be on her. There are some men not secure enough in themselves to be able to do that.

I look at the way being a man is defined in today's society and it seems to me so superficial and showy. Men think that they need to go to the gym, build these huge muscles and scream about how macho they are in order to be considered a man but that doesn't prove anything at all. It's like the core of real manliness has been taken away and now everything is a construction on the surface.

I think the same thing about femininity to an extent. There is so much more to being a woman than wearing a lot of makeup, putting on a dress and pouting. Femininity is about the way you move and speak and react with others; it's an almost indefinable quality. I can guarantee that a woman will never feel more like a goddess than when she is ballroom dancing, moving about in this incredibly womanly way, with a man whose sole job it is to make her look amazing.

Knowing all of this and taking this view on things, it always makes me laugh that people have a tendency to assume that male dancers are gay. Of course there are a lot of really talented gay male dancers out there in the world, but there are just as many who are straight and I would certainly fall into the latter category. As I said right at the beginning, as a little Siberian boy, beautiful girls had been one of the things that attracted me to dance in the first place! Having said that, I'm very much a 'one-woman' man. I don't really know how to play the field, it's never appealed to me. I'm in an environment with really attractive women every single day, but there are only a few where I've known that I wanted to take it a step further and pursue them romantically.

It just so happened that I met one such girl during the course of *So You Think You Can Dance*, although it was not Jessi, as everyone thought. I actually fell for one of Cat Deeley's stylists. Her name was Melis. We began talking on set and I just had that instinct of wanting to know more about her.

People often ask me what qualities I look for in a girlfriend and I find that really difficult to answer. I can only say that when I'm attracted to someone in that way I just know. I have a gut instinct about that person. So it was with Melis.

Both fortunately and unfortunately, we had signed an agreement with *So You Think You Can Dance* stating that we would not 'fraternise' with anyone else involved in the show. Since Melis worked for Cat Deeley and wasn't therefore technically part of the show itself or employed by Fox, we were not sure whether or not the rule applied to us, but we thought it was probably better to err on the side of caution and to try not to do anything that might get us in trouble.

The situation was unfortunate because it meant that we couldn't start dating properly or tell anyone else what was happening between us straight away, but it was fortunate because it gave us the opportunity to get to know each other slowly. While I was still part of the show, Melis and I were texting a lot. We didn't get the opportunity to spend a lot of time together face to face anyway, because I was rehearsing so much. My training schedule didn't allow me much time for socialising.

There was also the obstacle of our 10pm curfew. All of the *So You Think You Can Dance* contestants had to be back at the apartment complex by then. There were guards outside the main gates to stop anyone from getting in but that also meant that we weren't allowed out after that time. That didn't stop me from sneaking out a couple of times, James Bond style! On those occasions, Melis and I would do simple things like go and sit on the beach and talk for hours while looking at the stars. Another time we drove around to all her favourite spots in Los Angeles so she could tell me why she loved them so much and introduce me to her version of the city. It was all quite romantic, old fashioned and innocent.

By then, Anya and I hadn't been together as boyfriend and girlfriend for four years. I didn't have any other serious relationships during that time, but I still didn't feel that it was right to jump into anything headfirst. But, by the time the semi-finals of *So You Think You Can Dance* rolled around and it was announced that I would be going home, I found that a big part of the relief I felt was that I knew I'd now be able to spend more time with Melis.

When Anya returned to the show for the final and we saw each other for the first time since she'd been sent home, we suddenly found ourselves negotiating new territory. Anya had never seen me romantically involved with a girl other than herself. I felt that this, along with the fact that I had survived longer in the competition than she had, meant a distance between us was starting to grow. Definitely there was an emotional gap that hadn't been there before we had competed in the show.

In spite of that, both Anya and I had agreed to take part in the *So You Think You Can Dance* live tour and there was never any question of our not continuing as dance partners. After the tour, which lasted a couple of months, Anya told me that she was moving to Los Angeles. That was where all the on-going work and television opportunities would be, she said. I thought it was a good idea for me to do the same. By then, I'd seen a different side to LA and had grown to love the city. It was nice to know that was where Melis lived and that, when I moved, I'd have my girlfriend already there.

Everything seemed to be coming together and my new life on the other side of the TV divide was beginning.

Chapter 20

THE FAME
GAME

Ever since I appeared on *So You Think You Can Dance* back in 2007, I have been recognised wherever I go. However, I find that I have been able to maintain quite a nice level of fame to date, in that I don't have to worry about being mobbed. Some celebrities have to have decoys and take private cars everywhere, but I've never had to do any of that. I am occasionally photographed by paparazzi when *Strictly Come Dancing* is actually on air, but I never feel that their interest in me gets particularly invasive.

I can still use public transport without having to worry that the attention I attract will get out of hand. Just the other week, I was walking from the Tube station to a friend's house in east London. Getting there involves walking alongside a big main road and, on this occasion, a lot of congestion caused a traffic jam. A lady and her husband sat waiting in a car, facing in the opposite direction to the one I was walking. The lady had a small dog sat on her lap and, as I walked past, she said into the dog's ear, 'Oh, look! It's Pasha!' and then grabbed the little dog's paw to make it wave to me. I waved back and laughed. This kind of thing is typical of the sort of attention I get and it's generally nice in its nature.

It's strange because fame was never something I set out to achieve or that really appealed to me for its own sake, but now it has happened as part and parcel of my dancing career I have discovered that it comes with advantages. I don't mean the sort of advantages that spring to mind when you think of famous people, like being given free stuff or getting into exclusive clubs; I'm not motivated by any of that at all. It's more like being famous has allowed me to establish a bond with the public and to see myself through their eyes.

So often after appearing on television I was hearing from members of the public that they thought I was 'talented'. People would say it to me all the time. That was strange to me because I had never before thought of myself as possessing 'talent' in the traditional sense of the word. You remember I told you that when I first started dancing in Russia there was another boy in my studio who everyone described as 'talented'? The way he used to dance, he made it seem effortless, as if it just came naturally to him. He and others like him were the way in which my mind defined the concept of 'talented'. So, when I think of the word 'talent', it brings to mind someone who doesn't have to try really hard in order to be good at what he does. For that reason, I didn't ever think of myself as possessing a natural talent. The way I saw it, from a very young age I was deter-mined to make myself into a good dancer and every single day since then I worked really hard to make that happen. I found myself wanting to say to people, 'But if you practised every day for 20 years, you would be just as good as I am!'

At first, I thought it was kind of ridiculous that just because I was doing the job I did every day on television it was suddenly being described as a 'talent'. Simply because more people see you doing something does not mean you are any better at it than you were when fewer people were watching. Then I realised that by dismissing people's comments I was actually doing them a disservice. For them, there was no distinction to be drawn between the technicality of the dance I was performing and the story I was telling. It all came together in their perception of 'the dance'. If my performance moved and entertained them, and for that reason they thought I was talented, then who was I to argue?

My family back in Siberia aren't affected by my fame at all. They have a completely different entertainment culture in Russia and don't get a lot of American or British television. Even if that wasn't the case, my family and friends aren't the type of people to view me any differently simply because I am famous.

Without doubt, the weirdest time I was ever recognised in public was the very first time. *So You Think You Can Dance* had finished filming and I was back in New York City for a few weeks. I remember I went to see a film on 42nd Street. I love going to the movies and often go by myself; I don't see movie going as necessarily having to be a social activity – you're going to sit in the dark and watch a film, after all. So I was there on my own and I didn't think anything of it or factor in that I might get recognised. As I came out of the movie theatre, this girl, who must have been about 12, started jumping up and down and screaming, 'It's Pasha!'

The little girl asked if she could have a photograph taken with me and of course I said yes. There wasn't anything especially unusual about the encounter itself; it was only strange because it was the first time anything like that had happened and also because it was in a totally random place. Up until then, I'd always separated out my life as part of *So You Think You Can Dance* and my everyday life. It had genuinely never occurred to me that the two might overlap at any point. So, to just casually go to see a movie on a weeknight and have a fan of the show come up to me caught me totally by surprise.

After that, people started to come up and speak to me more and more. In a city like New York, you get used to the people who randomly talk to you on the sidewalk wanting something. It's not a place where people who don't know one another simply want to interact with each other for the sake of it. So, after a while of living there, when someone would say 'excuse me', you'd be instantly suspicious because you knew that, ultimately, they wanted cash or a cigarette, or something like that. I had to adjust to the fact that life wasn't like that anymore and people wanted to talk to me just because of who I was.

When people have watched you on the television, particularly if you have been part of a reality or talent show like *So You Think You Can Dance*, they get to feel as though they know you because they have shared in your life's journey. They've watched a part of your life story unfold and in the same way you have been part of theirs as you were on their television screen every Saturday night. Eventually, the viewer starts to think of you in the same way as they would a friend or family member. So, for

competition time!

Above: The third week of the *SYTYCD* competition. Me and Denny looking crazy!

Below: Getting ready for a group number with Sabra and Jaimie on *SYTYCD*, 2007.

Above: Everyone together on stage after Sabra was announced as the winner.

Below: I was lucky enough to go on tour with the *SYTYCD* team after the show finished. Here we are backstage!

Seing on *SYTYCD* opened up new doors for me, and I was invited to dance in the *Burn the Floor* production and tour the world!

Above left: With Mig in Melbourne, 2010. After a huge storm, piles of snow were all over the town, but it soon melted.

Above right: Sightseeing in Paris.

Below: Sydney harbour in 2010.

Above: Saint Martin in the Caribbean was beautiful. This is the first time I had ever been on a horse.

Below: From the hot to the cold: fishing in Aspen, Colorado, with my fishing guru.

tting ready to hit the slopes!

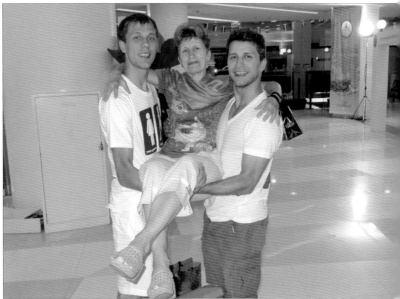

Even though I don't spend much time in Russia anymore, I still love to go home and see my mum. And, if I don't go to Russia, I like to take my mum on a little holiday.

Above: My brother, Mum and me in our hometown in 2011.

Below: In 2012, I took my mum to Thailand with my brother. She 'carried' us for a long time, now it's our turn to carry her. *All photographs © Pasha Kova*

ove being part of the *Strictly Come Dancing* family!

bove left: On the red carpet.

bove right: Katya was my dance partner when I joined the show – we make a eat team.

elow: With the cast on the *Strictly* live tour.

© Snooty Fox

them, it feels entirely normal just to come over and say 'hi' as if you have known each other for years.

In those situations, I'd always act like I might have met the person before until they said something that revealed to me actually we hadn't. I had been introduced to so many people since arriving in America that I was never sure whether I genuinely knew the person who was coming over to speak to me because everyone was acting as though they had seen me a million times before... which I suppose they had, just on television as opposed to real life.

Sometimes people would get overexcited. It was as if their brain could not compute that they were seeing someone in the flesh who they were used to seeing on a little box in their sitting rooms. I'd get people who would just freeze, mid-pace in the street. Others would start to shake.

That reaction of people being completely overwhelmed to see me still sometimes happens even today, although it is more rare than it was. It tends to happen more with younger people. As part of mine and Katya's live tour, each night we have a different local dance school come and perform a couple of numbers as part of the show. I love that element of the show – it's a way of actively engaging the local community in what we are doing and getting young people excited about dance, which is really important. I like to go and give the kids a little pep talk just before the show and express my appreciation of them for being part of it, usually while Katya is getting her hair and makeup done. Generally, they receive it really well but, on one or two occasions, one of the dance students has freaked out or looked like a little rabbit in the headlights when they have met me.

Then there are the people who react in the most peculiar ways to their interpretation of you as public property. I still find it really odd when a stranger asks me for a kiss. Or sometimes people ask for a photograph, which is cool but then, while it is being taken, they will try to grab my butt. I don't get why they think it's okay to do that or even feel as though it's something they want to do. Most women tell me they hate it when strangers pinch their butt in a club or something like that, so why are they then doing the same thing to me?

After I was recognised in public a few times, it dawned on me that I couldn't just do whatever I wanted without any prior thought anymore. I needed to be careful because there would always be eyes on me. I couldn't, for example, go out to a club, get really drunk and dance on a table because I wasn't simply 'Pasha' anymore – I was representing a brand wherever I went. Almost everyone has camera phones and Twitter accounts now. Anything you do can be released into a public forum within seconds, so you always have to bear that in mind.

When I was first grappling with the realities of fame, I knew I had to find some way to be a public version of myself whenever I was away from the confines of my own or a friend's house, but still be true to who I am. For me, it was more about being well behaved than anything else.

I wanted people to get to know the real me, just a version of the real me I could always be proud of.

Chapter 21

LOOKING FORWARD

The *So You Think You Can Dance* live tour was a completely different experience from the television show. I had gone from being in an incredibly fast-paced environment, where I had to learn and perform three or four brand-new routines every week to doing the exact same show every night, 50 times. I have to admit that after a while it got kind of boring.

I put the boredom I felt down, again, to the fact that I wasn't dancing with people trained in ballroom. Now, when I tour with Katya or another professional ballroom dancer, it never seems tedious at all because, even though we are still technically performing the same show each night, we are both confident enough in our art to keep it evolving and each performance maybe try out one or two new things. But dancing with people who didn't have a background in Latin or ballroom meant I had to stick rigidly to the same theme each time and I didn't feel like I was progressing as a performer.

All of us dancers who were part of the touring show did the same thing every single day. We'd spend the morning resting and recovering from the physical demands of the show we'd done the night before. Then we had a lunch, which had been prepared for us and brought to us. After that, we'd get ready for the show, do our stretches and change into our costumes. This was followed by the show itself. Then we'd go and do a meet and greet because, everywhere we toured, people would wait behind at the venue for the chance to have a talk with us and get our autographs. Afterwards, it was another meal, which we had late at night following the show, and then it was time for bed.

It was so weird to have ended up in this routine of just kind of floating along on someone else's pre-designed schedule when I had always been so independent in my life up until that point. I think how I grew up stood me in good stead, though, because a lot of the other contestants said they found it really hard to go back to their everyday lives and take care of themselves again after doing that tour.

We never got much of a break to do our own thing. When we weren't doing any of the activities described above, we were in the tour bus, travelling from place to place. Whole days and weeks seemed to run into one continuous journey across America.

I'll never forget the feeling of the tour bus doors being opened and stepping out to the sound of crowds screaming and hundreds of flashes going off as people took photos. It's the kind of thing you associate with being one of the Beatles or something like that. I genuinely felt like a rock star in those moments.

It's hard to describe the relationship that you build with the other contestants who are touring in that situation. We were all very friendly but it's not like you become best friends; you are just a group of people who happen to have been thrown into a situation together and of course you have fun and you get on, but there are no expectations that you will be best buddies for life. We related to each other because we had this shared life experience in common but, after the tour finished, we didn't have anything holding us together anymore and after a certain amount of time we all lost touch.

I remember in November 2012 I was rehearsing for *Strictly Come Dancing* and I realised that I hadn't brought a change of clothing to go and film their sister show, *It Takes Two*, straight afterwards. So, I went into Westfield London shopping centre, which is right next to what was then the BBC Television Studios in Shepherd's Bush, where the show was shot. I went into Diesel to pick up a shirt and was waiting at the cash register to pay when I noticed there was a guy standing next to me with a very distinctive and familiar haircut. His hair was shaved along one side but then on the other he had a spikey Mohican, sticking out to the side and going all the way down to below his ears. The only person I had ever known with that very unique haircut was a guy named Hokuto or 'Hok', an amazing street-dancer who was part of *So You Think You Can Dance* in the same season as me.

It turned out that he was passing through London and his luggage had got lost so he was in Diesel for the same reason as me: picking up some emergency clothing! I was happy to see him, but, after we had talked about what we were doing now (he had just starred in the video for 'Sexy And I Know It' by LMFAO), we didn't have anything else left to say to each other. We'd been so close and great friends while on tour together but now we just had a little catch-up before going our separate ways and getting on with our day. For me, that summed up the sort of relationship all the dancers had with each other on *So You Think You Can Dance*. We were on really good terms but our lives were only closely connected by the show and the subsequent tour.

After the *So You Think You Can Dance* live tour came to an end in November 2007, we were all going to have to make our own way in the world again, but of course being part of the show had brought us to the attention of a lot of people. I was left craving a project that would challenge me, something I could really sink my teeth into. That very opportunity arose in the form of *Burn The Floor*, a Broadway show boasting some of the most spectacular ballroom and Latin routines the dance world has ever seen.

Of course, starring on Broadway meant a move back to Manhattan for a while, but by that point Melis and I had split up so there was nothing keeping me in Los Angeles other than the fact that I loved the city itself. I think, looking back to when Melis and I first got together, everything was new and exciting and in a state of change. I got carried away with that, allowing myself to think that it meant she was the girl for me, when in reality we didn't have that much to build a relationship on. She is a great girl, but not right for me.

I don't think that Melis was expecting it when I told her that I was breaking it off. That's the thing about when relationships end – it's inevitable that one of you will have come to the conclusion that it isn't working before the other. When the break-up finally happens, it usually comes as a shock to one of the parties involved. That person might know that things hadn't been going well, but they didn't think it necessarily meant a break-up. In our situation, I was the one who had time to get comfortable with the idea of not being in a relationship anymore.

I'm the kind of person that if something isn't right then I don't hold onto it just for the sake of not changing things. It doesn't just apply to my relationships either. I'm the same with my jobs, my home and my clothes. All the time, I see people around me clinging onto things, whether they are positive or negative, because they are afraid to leap into the unknown and make a change in their lives. I have never been that way.

I guess my attitude probably stems from the way I was when I was growing up. I never had anything that really belonged to me and I was always moving from place to place so I learned from a young age that it's better not to become overly attached to things. That doesn't mean I don't care about the people in my life, just that I don't feel the same compulsion as others do to hold onto something once it has become toxic.

In the same way, I don't tend to look back. When I began writing this book, it was so difficult for me to recall the events that have made up my life in the necessary detail because I don't sit and reminisce, or endlessly go over things. I am a person who is always looking forward and completely focused on the next task at hand.

At that moment in my life, that task was taking me back to Manhattan and the chance to tread the legendary boards of Broadway.

Earlier, I mentioned that I didn't feel the need to be best friends with everyone on the *So You Think You Can Dance* tour because I already had best friends. At this juncture, I think it's important to mention the four best friends I have today (even though I didn't know all of them then) because they are such a key part of my life and my decision-making.

The four people I call my best friends could not be more different from one another. They are from four completely different parts of the world, with four completely different jobs and have four wildly varying outlooks on life. That is part of the reason I value their perspectives on what I'm doing so much – I know, between the four of them, they will cover every angle on a topic!

In order of when I met them, my first best friend is named Andrei and I've referred to him a few times throughout this book. Andrei is three years older than me and comes from a town a lot further north in Siberia. His hometown is so far north, in fact, that it's just an hour's flight away from Alaska.

Andrei was originally closer friends with Anya. His parents owned the first dance studio that Anya came from, before we all came together in the studio in the mining town in Siberia. In fact, despite Anya and I being in a relationship, Andrei developed a huge crush on her, so, when he called up from New York to invite us both to dance over in the States, the call was more for Anya and I just came as part of the package! But, after I arrived in the US, Andrei and I spent a lot of time together. He was showing me around and introducing me to his friends over there and we became very close as a result. Today, he lives in Atlanta and, as I said, he is one of my best friends.

My second best friend is named Alexei, but I call him Lyoha, which is his Russian nickname in the same way mine is Pasha, and he lives in Moscow. We met because, at the time I was living in Moscow, he was also a dancer and rehearsing in the same studio that Anya and I were using. At the time, I didn't have any close male friends and we just clicked straight away.

Lyoha really inspires me. Shortly after I moved to the States, he stopped dancing and started working with cars. He would source particular cars people wanted from all over the world and then he'd go and get that car for them, bring it back to Russia and take care of all the paperwork in return for a fee. He was so good at it that he was invited to work for car dealerships, initially in sales. Today, he is a regional manager and oversees all the car dealerships of his company in a huge area of Russia. To me, that shows how you can start with a simple idea and, if you work at it, you can turn it into something really successful and prosperous.

My third best friend is called Tolik. He is Russian but he lives in New York City today. I met Tolik in a completely random situation. I was living in New York but had travelled to Blackpool for a dance competition and while there I was hanging out with this girl. She introduced me to some friends and Tolik was among the group. He mentioned to me that he was thinking of moving to New York. My response was: 'Great! Give me a call if you get there,' but it was just one of those things that you say and I didn't really think anything of it.

A few months later, my phone rang. At first, I was like, 'Tolik? Tolik who?' but then he reminded me of how we met and I offered to show him round the city. As we spent more time together, I realised that we are completely different. We have opposing views on absolutely everything, from the big things (he's gay, I'm straight) to the small ones (I think it's important to take vitamins, he believes they are a waste of time). Through debating pretty much everything there is to debate, we became very friendly. I continue to be fascinated by Tolik's view of life today and can talk to him on the phone for hours.

My fourth best friend is called Nick. He is a casting director and he lives in Los Angeles. For a long time, he worked for MTV but now he has his own company.

Nick first saw me on the television when I was competing in *So You Think You Can Dance*. He sent me a message to my Myspace account at the time, telling me that he admired my skill. I don't remember that at all but Nick tells me it happened. Then, a few months later, I was introduced to him because he happened to be at a meeting Melis had to go to and I was tagging along. Again, I have no memory of that either!

Nick finally managed to lodge himself into my memory in the summer of 2008. I was hanging out with Andrei in Atlanta when I got a call from him to say that he was developing a show called *Dirty Dancing* (inspired by the film of the same name) and he really wanted me to be involved with the main choreographer. I said I couldn't do it because I was due to go back to Russia to see my mum in two weeks. He responded that I should go ahead and change my flights to Russia and back to fit in with the show, and they would take care of the related expense. I later found out that Nick paid for the tickets out of his own pocket because he wanted me to be involved so much.

Nick and I ended up travelling together to Los Angeles, New York City, Chicago and Miami, auditioning dancers for the show. We had a lot of fun, many nights out on the various towns and became firm friends. Today, I have my own room in Nick's house in LA, with my own bed that I bought. I do not have my own apartment over in LA anymore, so I think of Nick's place as my home.

I've stayed in touch with these four very different people and they have all played their own part in shaping my life. If ever I need advice, they are the ones I will call. I make sure I speak to all four of them and then I am confident that I have the whole picture on whatever decision I am making. The only thing Andrei, Lyoha, Tolik and Nick have in common is me. They have never been in a room together, all four of them. Their backgrounds, lifestyles, educations and perspectives are completely different from one another.

Sometimes, we get caught up in life and I will end up not communicating with one of them for a few months. That's how I know they are real, lifelong friends. We can always pick up right where we left off.

No matter where life takes us, we are always on the same page.

Chapter 22

BURN THE
FLOOR

It was October 2009 when Anya and I began performing as part of the cast of *Burn The Floor* on Broadway. Whenever I was doing press interviews at the time, the interviewer would always ask me the same question. They'd say something along the lines of, 'And how does it feel to be on *Broadway*?' with this big look of expectation on their faces. I was never sure how to answer. It was the show itself that excited me more than the theatre in which it was being performed.

The name 'Broadway' evokes so many things in people's minds. It has a completely iconic status for almost everyone, whether or not they are involved in the entertainment industry. A lot of people believe it's the greatest thing an actor or dancer can ever add to his or her résumé. From an outside perspective, there are so many people who have assumed that every actor, dancer and musician is walking around fixated on the idea of doing Broadway the whole time.

I can honestly say that 'treading the boards' of Broadway had never really entered my thoughts or been one of my life's ambitions, but once there I was very happy to be doing it. I suppose the situation was similar to how things panned out with *So You Think You Can Dance*. I never imagined myself doing a television show either and look what happened!

Having said that, I was aware that I was lucky to have this latest opportunity. I knew it was a dream come true for so many actors and dancers to have their names in lights in such a renowned location. People work their whole lives to get that chance. It's the same with performing in the West End of London. There are people who wait tables or work in jobs they hate for years and years just to get that one shot at performing somewhere that is seen to be at the centre of theatre's culture.

The reason I felt it was the right decision to perform in *Burn The Floor* was because it is purely a ballroom and Latin show; most Broadway productions incorporate a mixture of dance styles. Having said that, I knew that the routines we would have to learn would challenge me – the dance numbers had a reputation for being absolutely spectacular. I would have to draw on my experience from *So You Think You Can Dance* and go outside the boundaries of traditional ballroom and Latin routines to evolve the traditional dances into something new and exciting. Yet it was still fundamentally a ballroom show and, once again, I was keen to immerse myself in that world.

It's difficult to know how a show like *Burn The Floor* will be received. It has toured the globe to generally great reviews from the critics. There are few people who go away from watching *Burn The Floor* thinking it wasn't a really great, entertaining show. Having said that, if people are just in town and picking a theatre production to watch at random, what are the chances that they will choose a ballroom dancing show? I didn't know how they were going to make the appeal of what we were doing broad enough to entice the audiences in.

Kristina Rihanoff and Robin Windsor, two of my fellow professionals on *Strictly Come Dancing*, starred in the show in 2013, at the Shaftesbury Theatre in London. They were competing with shows that are just down the road in the West End, like *Wicked* and *War Horse* – huge institutions that everyone in Great Britain has heard of. So, they have done really well to carve a niche for themselves and to maintain the show's survival for all that time in the face of such competition when the production consists pretty much solely of dance numbers.

For the exact same reasons, I wasn't sure how long my life as part of the cast of *Burn The Floor* would last. I knew that what we were producing was of fantastic quality, but I couldn't anticipate whether or not audiences would want to see two hours of ballroom, or if they'd prefer just to go and see a play.

Broadway is full of tourists who are just wandering around, looking for something to do on their vacations. If they go to see a show, half the time they end up doing so completely by accident. More often than not, they will spot a poster for something or they'll go to the ticket office to see what production still has seats left, rather than having a definite idea of what they'd like to see in advance.

Anya and I were initially signed up for a three-month contract with *Burn The Floor* and that was good enough for me. I'm not the sort of person who has to know what he's doing months and months from now, and it was enough to have been involved in a show with such an incredible reputation for spectacle and excellence, however short a time it was going to last. As it turned out, the first three months Anya and I were involved with the show sold out, so we were signed up for another month. Then that month sold out so the same thing happened again. What was meant to be a three-month run ended up turning into six, and then it was time to embark on a world tour. Anya and I agreed to stay on and travel round the globe with the show.

Our first stop on the world tour was to be Melbourne, Australia.

I should have been excited at the prospect of getting to see more of the world and to carry on dancing in *Burn The Floor*, but at the time my head was in a strange and dark place. In the weeks immediately prior to flying out to Australia, I had begun dating a girl I really liked. As we headed out there, I was euphoric about being in love but, once I arrived, she phoned me and finished things. She'd been on the rebound after recently splitting with her ex-boyfriend, I believe, and told me she had gone back to him. I had my first ever experience of being truly heartbroken over a girl.

When that happened, I had never experienced anything so painful in my life before. There I was, starring in the most amazing show, with my name in lights, enjoying a fantastic career doing what I loved day after day, and what should have been a happy time was overshadowed by what was happening in my romantic life.

During *Burn The Floor*, I had to dance to a very sad song called 'Burn For You' with Anya. We'd dance a contemporary rumba barefoot to this beautiful, emotional track. Every time I danced it, I was thinking about the girl who broke my heart – it was like a daily reminder of what had happened.

I realised that I needed to change if I was going to be happy. After all, I was the only person who could have a positive impact on the situation I had found myself in and claw my way out of this emotional hole. That was when my whole view on what a relationship is, and should be, was transformed. I continue to live my life according to the values I arrived at during that period to this very day, more of which later.

I didn't know it at the time, but in flying to Melbourne I was about to undertake a journey that would completely alter my perspective on life.

To this day, Melbourne remains the cleanest city I have ever set foot in. There is a garbage bin every 10 feet as you walk down the street, meaning no one ever litters. Of course, there are other places in the world just as strict about keeping everything really tidy, but, in my experience, they don't have the same vibe as Melbourne. The whole town is incredibly peaceful and laid-back. In many ways, it reminded me of Los Angeles, but the vibe was even more relaxed than it had been over there.

Melbourne is a tranquil city and it's very pretty to look at. There is lots of modern and unusual architecture, interspersed with sculptures and huge monuments, yet the impression that you are left with after leaving is more to do with the people themselves than the infrastructure of the place. When I think back and picture the inhabitants of Melbourne in my mind, everyone is always smiling.

Melbourne could not have been more of a contrast to where I'd just come from: New York City. If someone passes you on a New York street, you are treated more as an obstacle getting in someone's way as they try to get on with their day. In Melbourne, people acknowledge you as a human being. There is a lot of social interaction on the street, just simple things like people saying 'good morning'. Generally, everyone acts as though they have all the time in the world and anything they might have to do that day can wait while they live in the moment.

So You Think You Can Dance US season three, the one in which I had competed, was the first to be aired internationally, rather than just at home in the States. There is an Australian version of the show too, but the Australian people were also able to watch the US version during the year I'd been involved, so when I got to Australia I found that there were people there who already knew who I was.

After we had been in Melbourne for three weeks, Anya and I were actually invited to go over to Sydney and do a live performance on *So You Think You Can Dance Australia* and to help with some of the choreography for the contestants that week, simply because we had fans over there. It was strange, the thought that there were people already aware of Anya and me and our dancing across the globe.

Australia is a place with a real appreciation for the art of ballroom dancing. One of my favourite movies about ballroom dancing, *Strictly Ballroom*, is actually set there. In fact, travelling around the world made me realise that it doesn't matter where you go, people always find a way to relate to ballroom. It's like an international language that everybody can understand. Of course different cultures pick up on different things within the dance, but it's safe to say I have never been anywhere on earth where the people of that place haven't found something that communicates to them within the act of ballroom.

My clearest memory of Melbourne is of a huge thunderstorm we had one evening, just before we were due to do the show. We went over to Australia in February 2010, which is summer in the Southern Hemisphere. Something to do with the warm air coming in had made these huge chunks of ice stick together and form in the air and now they were falling down to the ground in a freak storm.

Anya and I were due to perform in a big development in Melbourne's centre called the Crown Entertainment Complex with a theatre, cinema, casino and a shopping area. As we were doing our matinee performance all the rooms began to flood. We worked through it as much as we could but it got to the point where everyone needed to be evacuated so we had to take off our shoes and walk out of the building.

When we got outside, the storm had already passed and it was sunny again, but we saw there were some gigantic pieces of ice that had fallen out of the sky. They had crashed down onto parked cars and the sidewalk. It was like something out of a movie; the cars were covered right up to the windows with water, which was travelling at high speed downhill. Yet, everyone seemed to be really casual about it. We still went on to perform the show later that evening and the audience braved the weather to turn up. It was as though these spectacular meteorological conditions hadn't happened.

As I have already hinted, I was undergoing a personal transformation while out in Australia that dominated my experience and memories of the trip. I was trying to pull myself out of the misery I had been feeling after my recent break-up. In order to do this, I knew that I had to change the way I viewed things and move forward.

I embarked on another voyage of self-discovery. Around this

time, I started to meditate a lot and tried to get in touch with a calm, spiritual side of myself that would help guide me through this difficult time. I'd read a book that mentioned meditation, and I wanted to feel cleansed, calm and centred in a way that would allow me to see things clearly.

It was around then that I started eating less meat, too. I got talking to a nutritionist named Nikki out in Melbourne, who had previously worked with the cast of *Burn The Floor*. She advised me to start eating more fresh produce that would give me the energy I needed to dance without making me feel sluggish. I had a sit-down session with her and she drew up a plan that involved me eating millet and salad for breakfast and then lots of fresh fish throughout the day. Today, I still broadly stick to the plan that Nikki made for me.

With my new diet and a fresh outlook on life, I was starting to feel different in myself. I was able to get things clearer in my mind and to form some guidelines about the kind of person I wanted to be. I realised that all relationships are to an extent about dependency and getting the balance of dependency between the two of you just right. A lot of people put all their power and energy into someone else, thinking that person will be the one to make them feel fulfilled and complete. Many people – and I had also been guilty of this in the past – believe there's something fundamentally wrong with them and they seek a romantic partner to make them better. I realised, out in Australia, that we are already 'better': we don't need someone else to complete us, and going into a relationship thinking you do is not the basis for a healthy dynamic.

It's a cliché but I found truth in the words 'if you cannot be content on your own then you won't find happiness with anyone else'. If I was discontent, then I needed to be the one to sort that out. I couldn't go around thinking a girl would provide the magic solution to all of my problems.

I needed to have that first experience of being heartbroken in order to arrive at the conclusions that I did. It happened to be this particular girl whom I met and fell in love with before the tour who gave me the gateway to the thought processes I had in Melbourne, but it could just as easily have been anyone else. That too was an important conclusion to arrive at because it made me realise that the biggest reasons why I was so upset about our break-up were the imaginary ones I had imposed upon myself.

I'd created an illusion, based on my own expectations of what might have happened with this girl. In other words, I'd allowed myself to become upset by what I didn't have. It's just as dangerous as allowing your happiness to be based on the things you do have, which can just as easily be taken away. I decided that the reasons why I was in a bad place emotionally were of my own making; I'd put imaginary emotional obstacles in front of myself rather than deal with the real situation that I had.

Now, I believe that your state of happiness cannot have contingencies. What I mean by that is, if you say, 'I am happy because I have this thing and that thing,' then there is always the possibility that whatever it is that is making you happy can be taken away. From then on, I made a resolve that it would be me who had the power to decide how I handled things and how content I'd be.

It's just the same with those big blocks of ice falling out of the sky. Sometimes things happen which seem to indicate that the show can't go on and the easiest thing would be to give up.

But that episode where the people of Melbourne reacted so calmly and just got on with the day they had planned, regardless of the weather, showed me that you can choose how you deal with something that in another person's mind might be viewed as disastrous.

When my life was subject to unexpected weather conditions, it would be me who would decide that the show would go on.

Chapter 23

JAPAN AND KOREA

After Melbourne, the next stop on the world tour was Japan. For a long time prior to writing this chapter, I was trying to find another word to describe the fans Anya and I had in Japan that didn't involve saying the word 'crazy'. 'Crazy' has bad connotations for a lot of people, but, in applying it to the audiences when we took *Burn The Floor* to Japan, I mean it in a really good way. The people who turned up to our shows in Japan were without a doubt crazy, but it was a good, really endearing and fun-sort-of-crazy. I have never seen such enthusiasm and generosity.

Every single show we performed in Japan sold out and they always took place in a gigantic theatre space with room for a huge audience. The Japanese generally take art and culture much more seriously than we do over in the West. For them, dance isn't just entertainment, it has a deeper and more spiritual meaning. Before we began performing at any particular venue, religious leaders from the local town would perform a ceremony to bless the stage. They'd burn leaves and offer foods to their gods, asking for the show to go well and for no one to get hurt. Each ritual would be performed twice, once to stage left and once to stage right. I've never seen anything like it before. I was fascinated by the spectacle and took video footage on my camera phone to show friends back at home.

So You Think You Can Dance season three had aired in Japan, just as it had in Australia, so again Anya and I had a ready-made fan base waiting for us over there. Our fans would turn up before the shows with sweets and chocolates as gifts for us. You can probably guess how happy that made me. I discovered I had a favourite. It was called a *mochi* and was a sweet rice cake made of rice flour and filled with red bean paste. Absolutely delicious!

I fell in love with all the traditional Japanese sweet treats that the fans introduced me to. There are literally thousands of different varieties over there in all the combinations you can think of. Some of the flavours they put together were really unusual. Most of the time I didn't even know what it was that I was tasting. The only thing I knew was that I liked it!

In the Japanese department stores, there would be shelves and shelves of sweets everywhere you looked, with thousands of different varieties to choose from. I'd spend whole afternoons wandering around the stores, trying to work out what was in all the sweets because of course the descriptions were not in English and everyone spoke Japanese. There wouldn't be one familiar-looking chocolate in among the whole lot, so in the end I'd just have to buy something at random and eat it to see what it could be. With every mouthful, I embarked on a little adventure.

Some of the flavours weren't so great. Wasabi ice cream probably wasn't one of my favourites. I remember thinking, Why would you even think that was ever a good idea? But I was opening myself up to all these new taste sensations so I couldn't complain.

Everything about Japan was sweet. When we arrived in the country, the sakura cherry blossom trees were in bloom. Great expanses of parkland would be covered in cherry blossom and it was one of the most breathtaking sights I had ever witnessed. The flower is intensely pink, with a really powerful, beautiful fragrance that just gets everywhere. At certain times of year, the whole country smells of it. When the cherry blossom is out, there will be national holidays and festivals during which people will dress up to celebrate their national flower. It's quite something.

When I remember our time in Japan, I'm always struck by three things: the audiences, the beautiful cherry blossom landscape and the chocolates. Oh, *and* the toilet seat that warmed itself! I remember being struck by the genius of that. All the toilets over there had a little set of buttons and a remote control so you could select which direction the spray went in and whether you wanted wash or dry functions. My friends in the West always think it sounds strange to have a pre-warmed, intelligent toilet seat but I thought it was pretty cool. It would have been so nice to have one of those in freezing-cold Siberia when I was growing up!

We spent a total of two weeks in Japan and after that *Burn The Floor* moved on to South Korea for a week.

Korea has a very youthful spirit about it. Even though it is a place with a lot of history spanning many decades, you are still left with the impression of youth. Everyone has a lot of energy; they seemed to me to be sprightly in their movement and full of life. I remember that it seemed as though everyone I met was really young, although there must have been lots of different ages now I come to think about it.

My first couple of days in Korea I was really hungry. In Australia, I'd made the decision to start eating less meat and all of the Korean dishes are really heavy on it. There's just so much meat on menus in Korean restaurants but very little else. I'd made a commitment to change the way I was eating, and I didn't want to go back on that, but I was getting really grouchy from feeling hungry the whole time. That was until I discovered what happens there after midnight.

Every night at around 11pm, two or three huge tents would appear in the street right in front of our hotel. One evening, I went for a walk to explore and that's when I discovered that these tents are where the locals converge each evening to chat and eat. It's a little like a pub or a bar in the West, I suppose, but less focused on drinking and more on food and social interaction. They were absolutely amazing, these tents, with stalls selling fresh seafood and fish cooked to order, however you wanted it. Shrimp and octopus, two of my favourites, were for sale. After being so hungry, it was like an oasis in the desert!

I didn't know the language but I'd just point to whatever I wanted and then say 'yes' or 'no' as they held up various sauces and garnishes. Then I'd eat whatever I bought while chatting to the locals until about three in the morning. I always managed to run into a person who spoke a little bit of English and could translate for me. It was a fantastic way to bring together the community – more places should do it.

People would drink something that they'd call *ju*. Literally translated, it simply means 'alcohol' but what you'd normally get if you asked for it was something that looks and tastes like milk. It wasn't the custom to drink a lot of *ju* or to drink it to get drunk, just to enjoy a little with your food.

I remember some of the other dancers appearing in *Burn The Floor* went on an outing on our day off because they wanted to go and look at the border between North and South Korea. A lot of people think it's significant to do that because of course North Korea has a totally different political regime that is non-democratic and you're not allowed to cross over into their territory from the South. In fact, if you attempt to go over the line from either side, you will be shot.

You're not even allowed to get too close to the border and I just couldn't see the appeal in travelling all that way to look at a line from a distance. As far as I was concerned, I got to learn a lot more about the culture of Korea from my little midnight outings and observing and chatting as much as I could with the local people. Some of the locals were interested in the show and I'd talk to them about it as much as the language barrier would permit. Just visiting those tents on the streets after dark really made me feel as if I were part of something. It was like a small celebration of being part of a community, every single night.

I spent one week in Korea but those memories of socialising and eating with the local people will stay with me forever.

Chapter 24

A JAPANESE
ADVENTURE

This little adventure took place during the time when *Burn The Floor* was touring Japan. I like remembering this story because it gives a glimpse of the spirit of the people over there and also shows how life can give you little gifts, if you are open to receiving them.

I'd first developed a taste for sushi a few years after moving to the United States, while staying in Atlanta with my friend Andrei. Fresh out of Russia, at first I found the idea of eating raw fish appalling, but then Andrei dragged me along to a sushi bar and forced me to try it, convinced I'd enjoy it. I discovered raw fish to be much more pleasant than I'd imagined. After that, sushi became a regular staple for me. It's very important for dancers to eat a lot of protein in order to build and maintain lean muscle. The problem is that, if you get that protein from meat, it can leave you feeling heavy, sluggish and unable to dance your best, which defeats the object. Sushi is very light and you don't need a nap after you've eaten it. In fact, I find it gives me an instant energy boost, which makes it an ideal part of a dancer's diet.

One of the things I was most looking forward to about visiting Japan was the opportunity to sample real sushi. I'd been told that what they actually eat in Japan is quite different and far superior to what we consider to be sushi in the West, just as authentic Italian cuisine differs vastly from what you might be served in a pizza chain. I couldn't wait to see what it would be like.

So, imagine my disappointment when, while performing in the Japanese city of Osaka, I discovered that real Japanese sushi was actually quite hard to come by. For some reason, most of the restaurants seemed to be serving Korean dishes instead.

On my last night in Osaka, I decided it was silly to have come all this way and to leave without having sampled the sushi. I was on a mission, determined that, by the end of my stay, I would have found what I was looking for. As usual, I finished my last show at around 10pm and soon I was wandering the streets, searching for the elusive sushi I'd been craving.

There was only one place that seemed to be open, with its lights on. It was completely empty apart from one guy who worked there and was standing behind a long steel counter. I explained to him in English about my search and asked if he could help, hoping he'd be able to understand me. Luckily, he spoke some English and explained that I had actually wandered into a coffee house, but asked me to follow him into a dark, narrow alleyway outside.

I couldn't see to the end of the alleyway because it was so dark and the walls were close to me on either side, so that I could touch them both without fully extending my arms. Reading my words back, it sounds as if it could have been a scary situation, but I can honestly say that I didn't feel at all apprehensive about going after the coffee house guy. He didn't give me any reason to be scared of him. I did wonder what was about to happen, or whether he had misunderstood my English in some way, though.

A moment later, he gently pressed against one of the walls of the alleyway. I couldn't believe it when the bricks began to move. The magic wall slid to one side and revealed, to my delight, a tiny sushi restaurant situated just behind it.

The secret restaurant was so minuscule it consisted only of a small counter with a chef standing behind it and four stools. Already there were people sitting on three of the stools, leaving room only for me. The other three customers looked up as I entered, as though they had somehow been expecting me.

I had no knowledge of the Japanese language at that time. The only words I knew how to say were 'hi', 'yes' and 'thank you'. So I thanked the man from the coffee house and pulled up the last remaining stool. I figured I'd come this far and I just had to explore the magical little alcove further. After all, it's not every day that you get to see what goes on behind the hidden walls of a city. There's a whole concealed world behind the edifice of any city in the world you could visit, but very few have the privilege of experiencing it for themselves.

I only had a limited amount of cash with me. I'd budgeted for my entire trip to Japan as a whole and, as it was my last day, I was running low on cash in my pocket – this wasn't the sort of place that would take a debit card. But I figured I had enough for at least a couple of sushi pieces.

I quickly discovered that one of the guys sitting at the counter had gone to college in the United States and, as a result, spoke a little English. He kindly offered to help me order what I wanted and communicated with the other customers and the chef on my behalf. I had found an ally in an alley!

I told my new friend a little about the show I was dancing in and he translated for the others. He, in turn, told me that the little place in which we were sitting was the best sushi restaurant in town. The sushi chef, he said, was one of the finest in the world but he did not speak any English at all, so anything I wanted I'd have to ask for through him. I felt very excited to be in the presence of a chef who was obviously an expert in the field of sushi, so I instructed my friend simply to ask for 'anything that is good'.

Immediately, I was asked if I wanted *sake*, which is a traditional Japanese alcoholic beverage, served warm or cold in tiny cups. I was worried that adding alcohol to my meal would take me out of my price range, so I spread my cash out on the counter and said, 'If it completes the dinner, then yes, I'll have *sake*, but I can only drink up to however much I can get for this much money.' The *sake* was poured and I was confident they had understood.

I have noticed, whenever I have had to learn a new language, people never remember to teach you the names of birds, fish and animals. It's one of the last things you are told, even though it's essential learning because what you eat centres around knowing those names.

When I was first learning English properly in the States and people were saying the names of animals and birds to me, I'd have to Google them to see what they looked like, so I could understand what they were talking about. It's hard enough to describe animals when you don't know the English names for them, but virtually impossible to describe in words the difference between varieties of fish. So I understood how difficult it was for my new friend when he was attempting to let me know what I was about to eat in the sushi bar.

It's really funny, looking back and remembering him trying to describe a type of fish and me trying to guess what he could mean.

Tiny pieces of white fish came out for me first and I began to eat them. They were chewy and a little bitter to the taste. I still had no idea what I was eating, despite the best efforts of the other people in the restaurant, until the chef pointed with his knife over to the corner of the room, where a blowfish was on a rope hanging from the ceiling. I knew enough to know that if blowfish isn't cut and served exactly right then it can kill you, really quickly. Certain parts of the fish are highly toxic. I thought to myself, Wow, I really am finding out whether this man is a good sushi chef!

I was asked if I liked meat. Again, I just said to bring me anything that was good and they thought that I should try. This time, I was given something raw and red. It melted in my mouth and was delicious, much nicer than the blowfish. As I ate, the sushi chef started blowing raspberries and stamping his feet to indicate that I was eating horse. Although a little shocked because I had never expected to eat horse, at that point I thought it was the nicest piece of meat I'd ever eaten. I laughed at the chef's equine impressions, the *sake* he kept pouring out for me going straight to my head.

I suspected by that stage that I had gone well over the

amount of cash I had brought with me into the restaurant and made to go to a nearby cashpoint so that I could pay. The three other men gestured for me to sit back down. My English-speaking companion explained that they all felt strongly that I should not pay because I was a guest in their country. When I protested and said I wanted to pay what I owed, they became insistent and said they would not let me do so.

After two hours, I left that tiny, secret restaurant beaming from ear to ear. My first experience of real sushi had left me with a good feeling, not just in my stomach but also in my heart.

Chapter 25

JOURNEY'S
END?

After getting the chance to see some culture that was completely alien and contrasted with anything I'd experienced in Russia, Europe or America, it was time to head for more familiar terrain.

The next leg of the world tour took us to Canada. It wasn't the first time I had ever visited the country, but it was the first time I'd ever flown there after a world tour and I was seeing the place with new eyes. I remember thinking it was funny how the Americans joke about not liking the Canadians and vice versa, when after seeing the contrast with other parts of the world, they just seem like the same country. After we landed in Canada, at the end of April 2010, I remember having the distinct feeling that I had come home.

We spent a week in Vancouver, which is very different to Toronto, where we were based the rest of the time. I recall thinking how Vancouver is actually really similar to my original hometown, back in Siberia; it kind of looks the same. Certainly, the plants and trees you see outside are the same and a lot of it reminded me of the parks where I used to play as a young boy. It's also really cold in Vancouver in the same way as it is where I grew up.

All of our days off were spent travelling, which didn't leave us with any time to rest and recuperate. It was like a final sprint at the end of a long-distance run. Our schedule was becoming increasingly relentless and everything just blurred into one seemingly never-ending dance.

There were only one or two things I can remember doing in Canada apart from dancing in the show. One was visiting Niagara Falls. It's hard to describe what it feels like to stand beside something so awe-inspiring and powerful in nature. The Falls make you forget everything that exists around them. It's almost as if they draw you in and, once there, you have a sense of your own insignificance; you feel dwarfed by the magnificence of them.

Other than that, Canada – and Florida, to where we travelled next – became a bit of a whirlwind. We dancers were swept along by the momentum of the tour, with little of our own energy left to draw on. By then, we were so exhausted and drained. Having said that, I cannot claim that I was jet-lagged at any point during the world tour. When discussing my extensive travels with people, it's something I get asked about all the time. You don't have time to become acclimatised to a place and to adjust to their clock when touring with a show, you just have to turn up and start dancing. I think maybe because of that I have never suffered from jet lag. I hear people talk about the symptoms that you get when you become really unwell from jet lag – headaches and feeling sick and dizzy, for example – and I simply cannot relate to it at all. The most I have ever felt after travelling a long way is a little tired.

Even when I have time off, my tendency will always be to go out and do something rather than sit indoors and chill. When it comes to relaxation, I really don't do things by halves. I have a couple of days a year where I literally sit in my hotel room or apartment with the curtains drawn and just slouch about, watching movies. On those days, I will be too lazy even to get up and fetch myself some food. I just lie there, feeling hungry because I'm too lethargic to find the will to get up. The rest of the time, I am always active. I haven't yet got to grips with the whole art of 'chilling out'. Perhaps the day I stop to take a breath will be the one when it really hits me how exhausted I am! But, like I said, none of that mattered for the last leg of *Burn The Floor*'s world tour because we didn't have any time off, anyway.

After the world tour finished in Florida in May 2010, Anya and I were asked if we'd like to stay on for a tour of the United States. By taking part in the show, I felt that I was feeding in to something I truly loved; I didn't see any reason not to continue being part of the cast. Even though the training was really hard-core, I was content doing what I was doing. I enjoyed being part of the company and I got along with all the other dancers. It made sense to continue burning the floor! The American tour didn't begin until October, which also allowed me a little time to go back to Russia and see my family.

There was also a part of me that always knew that the *Burn The Floor* bubble had to burst at some point. As a dancer, you are always aware that you have a shelf life. Like any professional sportsperson, you cannot carry on forever. You might retire and then continue in the dance world, maybe as a choreographer or a teacher, and that has its own rewards but performing on stage gives you a high. There is no doubt that performance is like a drug and I'm certainly addicted to it. In many ways, it reminds me of the same feeling I get whenever I eat chocolate – it's intense and sweet to perform on stage and, after the sugar rush has died down, I know I will be left craving more. I wanted to do as much live performance as I could, before I wasn't physically able to do so anymore.

It wasn't long, however, before the *Burn The Floor* American tour started to feel like just a job to me. The excitement I'd felt when performing the show on Broadway and while travelling all over the globe began to dissipate. For me, the show had lost some of its magic. It was around this time that I got a call from the producers of *Dancing With the Stars*, which is the American version of *Strictly Come Dancing*.

I let Anya know that I had received the call and she asked what I was thinking. I answered her honestly: I wasn't thinking anything. This time, I needed a few days to digest the information and let it sink in. It was a decision I had to process in my gut, thinking about it would be futile.

It wasn't the first time that *Dancing With the Stars* had invited me to be on their show. In fact, they had first contacted me when I'd been performing *Burn The Floor* on Broadway and two further invitations had been issued since that first call. However, this particular occasion was the first time that the offer was made and my eventual response, after giving myself the time I needed to process, was to think, I am ready.

I knew I really wanted to be part of the television show, but

I'd already signed a contract with *Burn The Floor* that wasn't due to expire for another few months. Anya and I were headlining the show, so it wasn't as if I could leave inconspicuously to be quietly replaced with someone else. If I'm honest, there was a part of me that thought about just quitting *Burn The Floor* and taking the opportunity with *Dancing With the Stars* regardless of my contract. I certainly contemplated it and I took the step of discussing my potential departure with the team at *Burn The Floor*. Yet in the end I just couldn't justify it to myself, morally. I'd never been the sort of person not to see something through, and I did not want to start then.

Then of course there was Anya to consider. The invitation from *Dancing With the Stars* had not been issued to us both. Making the move away from *Burn The Floor* would mean breaking up our dance partnership, something that had lasted for over a decade. By the same token, since *So You Think You Can Dance* I had been feeling that Anya and I were on a different page. The closeness we once shared wasn't there anymore and something instinctual told me our dance partnership would have to break up at some point, whether now or in the future.

The logistics weren't right, however, for me to be able to fulfil my commitment to *Burn The Floor* and to seize the chance I now knew that I wanted with *Dancing With the Stars*. It was so frustrating to have that kind of carrot dangled in front of me and for my conscience to be holding me back, yet I was duty bound to do the right thing.

It seemed there was no way out of the situation. Then, in March 2011, another phone call came, offering me an alternative: it was from the makers of *Strictly Come Dancing*. It was easy for me to say 'yes' straight away and without hesitation when invited to become part of the team on *Strictly Come Dancing*.

I'd already done all the soul searching and gone through the process of thinking through what I wanted when *Dancing With the Stars*, *Strictly*'s sister programme in the States, approached me a few months before. I felt strongly that performing on television, in a role that also allowed me to use my skills as a dance teacher, was the right way to go and I was just so pleased that the opportunity was being given to me. It was like a gift from life!

By the time I was making the *Strictly* decision, Anya was already not talking to me. After I had told her how much I wanted to accept the offer to be on *Dancing With the Stars*, she made it very clear that she would see the breaking up of our dance partnership as a betrayal. Then, of course, all the residual feelings she had about it being her original ambition to dance on television and the opportunity being given to me were thrown into the pot. What emerged was one angry Anya!

It was so strange because she and I were still dancing together every single night on *Burn The Floor*, but backstage she wouldn't so much as say hello to me. After a couple of weeks, she softened up a little and began to acknowledge that I existed, which was better, but by then there was so much distance between us, emotionally, that I didn't even discuss my decision to go over to *Strictly Come Dancing* with her at all.

I suppose at one point there was a naïve part of me that had convinced myself there would be a way to incorporate Anya into my future in Britain. Maybe she could travel over with me and we could perform in live shows together when I wasn't filming, I thought. I had a couple of loosely formed ideas like that. The idea of her coming with me was a possibility that I briefly spoke about. Her response was: 'If you go, then I am sure we will never dance together again.'

Anya couldn't have found a more precise way to express how she felt. At that point, I knew for certain that we would be going our separate ways from then on. I realised that the prospect didn't scare me or bother me in any way. I was sorry that Anya was taking the news so badly but, when I examined my own feelings, I realised that I felt free. Our working relationship had been stormy for a long time. It seemed that Anya was always so opinionated about how we should be dancing and where we should be doing it. If she didn't like my ideas, they were dismissed; I felt there was no flexibility or compromise in the dynamic between us. It was stressful, living every day that way.

I'd accepted things being like that between Anya and me for a long time but, suddenly, knowing there was no way we could maintain a professional relationship, I was released from the situation. When we first started dancing, Anya had balanced me. Back then, I had needed someone driven and in control. I realised now the dynamic between us had changed: I was different from before, whereas it seemed Anya had remained the same.

In breaking up our partnership, I was suddenly in a position where I didn't have to check with Anya every time I made a decision. I was at liberty to do whatever I wanted. And the first thing I wanted to do was to use the little time I had off between *Burn The Floor* and *Strictly* to go home to Siberia to see my family.

This wasn't the first time I had been back to Russia since

moving over to the States. That initial time I talked about before was when I was so shocked by the contrast in the culture over there after what I had grown used to in America. Now I knew what to expect and I could completely focus on spending time with my mum and brother.

My brother Sasha is almost a decade younger than me so, when I returned to Russia in 2011, it was really the first time he was old enough that we could hang out together as adults and I could properly get to know the person he was. It was brilliant to both be adults and to be able to relate to each other in ways other than simply having the same parents.

Sasha introduced me to some of his friends and we hung out and played pool with them. When we weren't doing that, we spent hours just talking. We talked about all aspects of life – work, love, the universe, everything.

Sasha talked about how he had taken some dance classes as a young boy and how his teachers had said he had quite a natural talent for it. In the end, though, he had been put off by all the politics that went on in the dance studio. He hadn't felt that he was treated properly, so he had given up on dancing around the age of 12 and confessed to me that he wished he had been more persistent.

While living in Moscow, before I made the move to the States, I had called my mum and said there was the opportunity for Sasha to join me in the city. I don't think that Mum ever told him about that conversation. It would have been really difficult for her, had both her sons moved away from home. Having said that, she would never have prevented Sasha from doing anything that he was determined to do. If he had a clear idea of what he wanted, Mum would have been as supportive of any decision he made as she was of mine to go away to dance school. The truth is, as I write this book, Sasha is aged 25 and still unsure as to what career path he wishes to follow. He takes jobs to pay the bills, but he is still waiting to find his niche. Which is fine – not all of us find it when we are eight!

Sasha and I spoke a lot about how our hometown had changed since the introduction of democracy. The place had become really introverted and stagnant, with everyone working in a different shop and all those shops buying goods from one another. I could see how it would seem as if there was no outside world when you lived there. Now, when I see my family, I like to do so elsewhere. It isn't simply that I find my hometown a little depressing, it's my way of treating the family and giving them a share of my success.

Recently, I took my mum on holiday to Thailand, for example. It was her first experience of a hotel and she was so excited by it. We were right next to the ocean and she had never seen anything like it before in her life. Watching her take so much pleasure from something I'd been able to provide gave me a lot of pleasure. I asked Mum where she wanted to go next time and she decided on St Petersburg. I'm taking her there soon.

I suppose we all have this in-built desire to provide a better life for our families. I remember, as a little boy, I used to tell my grandma that when I was older I would buy her a fur coat. She died when I was 15 and I was left feeling as if I never got the chance to show her how important she was to me. I don't mean simply by giving her material things and finally getting her that coat, but because I was away at school I didn't get to spend that much time with her, either. So now, whenever my schedule allows, I like to see my mum and to do that somewhere it will be a treat for her to visit.

After going back to Russia, I returned briefly to Los Angeles and to the set of *So You Think You Can Dance* as an 'All Star'. An All Star is a dancer from a previous season who returns to the set to dance with one of the current contestants, who has picked their style to dance that show. We help the contestant with technique and getting used to choreography, then perform the routine with them at the end of the week.

I loved the experience of being an All Star. This time I wasn't a choreographer and I wasn't a contestant, I was somewhere in between so I didn't feel any of the stress; I was just there to help and feed into the creative process. I got to dance and help create some amazing routines: It was a little like my own days in the competition in that I was challenged by a new routine and under pressure to perform it well, but I was doing all this in a much more relaxed frame of mind. For me, it was a perfect balance.

After that, it was time for my *Strictly* journey to begin and so in August 2011 I boarded a plane towards a new chapter of my life in Merry Olde England.

Chapter 26

LONDON
CALLING

Long before England was even on the cards for me, a psychic predicted that I'd end up living in London for a while.

Anya and I were living in Los Angeles at the time and, one day, she came up to me really excited, telling me about this amazing man she'd been to see who had predicted her future. I'd never done anything like that before, but Anya was so sure that this guy was credible and accurate that I decided to give it a shot, just to see what it would be like.

When I showed up at the address Anya had given me, it was just a completely regular-looking house in the middle of suburbia. Then the guy answered the door and he looked more like how I'd imagined a lawyer to look than a psychic. I realised I'd been expecting someone who looked like one of the wizards out of *Harry Potter*, with long hair and a robe with stars on it.

I also expected him to use tarot cards or maybe a crystal ball. At the very least he'd make a magic potion or go into a trance. Like I said, I'd never done this before so I guess I was basing my assumptions on some stereotypical notion I had of what a psychic is like from books and television. Yet, when I stepped into his office (which again was just a normal sort of room with a desk, chair and computer), he simply asked me for a couple of details, such as my date and place of birth. At that stage, I thought perhaps he would do some maths based on the facts I had given him, but he actually just looked at me and started to talk.

One of the things the psychic told me was that he saw me moving to London for a couple of years. I'd never been to London before as my trips to Britain had always involved going to Blackpool for dance competitions, so I just couldn't picture it at the time. Then, a little while later, here I was travelling to England. I still don't know whether maybe I just had London in the back of my mind from the point when I visited the psychic, so subconsciously I made it happen, but there's no denying, whichever way it was, the prediction came true.

I was really enthusiastic about the prospect of exploring London, a city with such a rich cultural heritage. Even though it was August when I arrived in England and supposedly the middle of the summer season, I'd been warned not to expect any sunshine. Friends who had visited before told me that London is 'a city of rain' with a constant grey skyline. In fact, as I write this, it is May, which should herald the beginning of summer, and I'm actually looking out of the window at a cold, grey skyline so I can't pretend there's no truth in what they told me! But, when I first arrived in London in August 2011, my initial experience of the weather was the complete opposite of what I had been told.

The city was in the midst of a heat wave. The sun was shining so fiercely in the sky that, everywhere I went, I heard people complaining that it was too hot! As it turned out, that year the sun continued to shine right through the summer months and lasted until what should have been the autumn. I was loving the climate – it meant the transition from Los Angeles, with its consistently beautiful blue skies, was so much easier for me. Only when I reflected back on it afterwards did it occur to me how much it seemed as if London was welcoming me in.

If you compare London to any other city I have seen on my travels, it is the first place that has really impressed upon me a sense of class and sophistication. Although the streets are tiny and narrow because they haven't changed since medieval times and a lot of the buildings are really ancient, London has this atmosphere of grandeur and importance. I got the impression that the city was perhaps quite a conservative, old fashioned sort of place compared to the relaxed, easy-going energy of LA, but there was also this cheeky, eccentric side to it.

When I think about my first impression of London, it always brings to mind the image of a quintessential British gentleman. In my head, he is dressed in a top hat and tails, carrying a cane. He'd have great posture and be really graceful in his movements, but he'd also be able to tell a really funny joke. If the character of the city was embodied into a person, they would be like that, I think.

I had it in my mind when I first got to the city that I'd use any time off to explore. London is a place that has all these little nooks and crannies hidden away from the main streets. At any one time, there are so many exciting things going on in some obscure little side street, somewhere off the beaten track. I wanted to wander around, get lost, soak up the atmosphere and see what adventures I could get myself into.

Little did I realise I wouldn't have any spare time! We began rehearsing the professional group numbers for *Strictly* pretty much as soon as I arrived. Each week during the show, the professional dancers perform a group routine on top of the routines danced with their celebrity partners. To save time and maximise the number of rehearsals we are able to do with our celebrity dance partners once the series began, the custom was to work out all the professional group routines in advance. We'd film the finished choreography so that when the time came to perform them during the course of the series all we had to do was remind ourselves and refresh what we had already learned.

When I wasn't in the studio, I was flat hunting. I'd booked myself into a hotel in Battersea when I arrived, but I couldn't stay there forever and I knew I had to try to figure out which part of the city I needed to be in to make my commute to the BBC Television Centre an easy affair. *Strictly* is filmed in west London so I figured I would start looking around there.

Every single day, I was going to look at these apartments in Marble Arch, Lancaster Gate and Notting Hill, which were all situated in the west of the city, within easy distance of the television studio. I must have seen hundreds of flats, or so it seemed. I couldn't believe how crazy the rental market was over in the UK. I wanted a short-term lease for the five months that I knew I would be in Britain filming the show and

I was being told that nothing was available to me for that amount of time without these insane financial conditions being attached because I didn't have any previous rental experience in the country.

Although I was still getting my head around what was a normal amount for things to cost, it also seemed to me that all the apartments in London were way too expensive for the size. I was looking at all these cramped, shabby little places and the landlord or landlady would tell me that they wanted an extortionate amount of monthly rental and, as a foreigner, I would have to pay the entire five months up front, plus a deposit.

I knew I wasn't going to be spending a lot of time lounging around in my flat once I found somewhere to live, but even so I wanted it to be nice enough that it felt like a retreat. Even if I was just laying my head there after a hard day of rehearsing, I needed my home to be somewhere I could truly relax. It was proving really difficult to find somewhere suitable.

I was expending so much time and energy in a search for a place to live that was yielding no results and getting really frustrated when my friend Wendy (the one from New Zealand, who makes the most amazing shepherd's pie that I mentioned earlier) provided me with a lifeline. She knew of a lady specialising in short-term leases for people in my position. This woman made a living out of buying up properties and then renting them out to friends of friends from all over Europe and across the globe. Luckily, I was a friend of her friend and so I soon found myself in an apartment that met my requirements.

Now I was settled, the time had come to do some exploring, I thought. Finally, I could really get to know London. Except that was when we were told which celebrity we'd be dancing with for *Strictly*. As it turned out, my partner for the series lived 200 miles away, in Manchester.

Chapter 27

THE SIEVE

The first day I walked into rehearsals for the professional group routines on *Strictly Come Dancing* I had no idea what to expect. Of course I was aware of the show, but, coming from the States, I hadn't actually sat down and watched it. I knew *Strictly* was where it had all started and that the show had given birth to the *Dancing With the Stars* franchise over in America. Back in the US, I had caught *Dancing With the Stars* a couple of times on television and had even done a little choreography for them in the past so I knew broadly what *Strictly* would be about, even though I understood the format was a little different. Yet I wasn't familiar with the various characters who made up the *Strictly* cast or what my new environment would be like as a result.

It was a bit daunting, the idea that I was going to have to walk into a room full of the people with whom I would be working in such close proximity for the next five months and to introduce myself to them, just like that. As it turned out, I had no reason to worry. I already knew four out of the 14 *Strictly* professionals and the ones I didn't know couldn't have been nicer or more welcoming.

I thought it was funny that I immediately saw so many familiar faces and I was struck by what a small world the dancing business is. Kristina Rihanoff, who everyone knows as the sexy bombshell with the Marilyn Monroe hairstyle on the show, I have actually known since I was a little boy. We both come from the same region, back in Russia, and I always used to see her at the regional dance competitions. We'd never actually competed against one another because Kristina always used to dance with partners who were a little older than me and were therefore competing on a different level back then. After that, just like me, Kristina had moved to the United States and our paths crossed a few times while I was living there, so she was definitely a familiar face.

I had known Artem Chigvintsev in the States. Even though he is Russian, too, we had never met each other before I moved over to America. The girl he used to be married to was one of the cast members for *Burn The Floor* and then he had joined the show in time for the world tour. So we had actually spent a lot of time together in Australia, Japan, Korea and Canada, and we'd got into a couple of crazy adventures during our time off.

Aliona Vilani had spent some time dancing with Andrei, my friend who had called me when I was in Moscow to say they were looking for dancers over in New York City. Then, later on, she had been dating and dancing with another friend of mine who is a couple of years younger than me and actually from the same hometown in Siberia. He and I both started dancing at the same studio as little boys. I had a running joke with this particular dancer friend I am referring to because he and I looked incredibly similar. I remember once at a competition that I was going into the bathroom as he was coming out and I said, 'Hey, how can I be going out just as I am walking in?' We looked so alike that I had managed to confuse myself. He and Aliona eventually split up but I remember him telling me how fiery and passionate her character was. I was a little wary of her at the very beginning because I wasn't sure how this fiery nature I had heard about was going to manifest itself!

Bobbie – or Robin Windsor – who joined *Strictly* the year before I did was part of the Broadway cast of *Burn The Floor* so I'd already worked with him.

It's funny that I did not actually know Katya, with whom I was partnered that year and now dance with for our live tour, even though she is from the former USSR. I had seen her before, though, because she appeared alongside Antonio Banderas in the movie *Take The Lead* (2006). In it, Katya plays a kind of stuck-up girl who takes ballroom lessons with a private tutor, who is played by Antonio. I actually knew the real teacher on whom Antonio's character in the movie is based back in New York City, which is how I ended up going to see the film. In one scene, Antonio's character uses Katya's character's dance skills to show some kids he is teaching in a poorer area of the city that ballroom can be cool. Katya walks in to where they are gathered in a basement underneath their school and performs this really sexy tango with Antonio. It's definitely one of the scenes to stick in your mind. I remember asking my friend who was there watching the movie with me, 'Who is that girl?' and his reply being, 'Oh, just some Canadian!' (Katya moved to Canada when she was a teenager.)

The producers of *Strictly* told me that Katya would be my professional partner for that series and I later found out that she had specifically asked the BBC to pair her up with 'the new boy'. The guy she was dating at the time, Claus (who is now her husband), had been coached by Allan and Vibeke, who I've spoken about before, and owned one of the New York studios I danced in. In fact, Allan and Vibeke had inspired Claus to start dancing in the first place and he is now a world ballroom champion. So Katya asked Claus to ask Allan and Vibeke what sort of a guy I was, and apparently the report that came back was a good one. From then on, she decided she wanted to dance with me!

The first thing I ever rehearsed for *Strictly* was a number that was to be danced by Katya and me, as well as Brendan Cole and his professional partner for that series, Natalie Lowe. Katya had selected the music for the performance, which was Adele's 'Rolling In The Deep'. The routine was a foxtrot, mixed with a quickstep and it remains one of my favourite professional dances of that season. After rehearsals, I remember that Katya and I went for a curry to seal our friendship and discovered that we had lots of other contacts and friends in common.

Katya and I jelled really well immediately because we have a very similar approach, but that is tempered with a different set of skills. We're both very easy-going and calm and not precious about things so we don't devise a routine and then refuse to listen to other people's suggestions as to how it might be improved. Neither of us is a control freak in that way. Whereas I like to dance Latin and am more of a creative type, Katya

214

prefers ballroom and is very organised, so the BBC were really insightful to pair us together. We balance each other well and that's why we decided to perform a live tour together after the show had finished filming.

In 2013, I did another tour with Katya and I can only ever remember arguing with her once in the whole time we have been dancing together. It was when she really wanted to dance to a song by Michael Bublé called 'I'm Your Man' but I just wasn't feeling it. I think Michael Bublé has a beautiful voice but it wasn't a number that inspired me to move in the way that I needed to in order to perform the dance. Music is really important to the way the storyline of a dance routine comes across and I think we were each hearing a different message within the song and it meant that the performance wasn't coming together. Katya was trying to get me to express her meaning of the song through the steps and I had to say to her, 'That's not what the music is telling me.' That's really the closest thing to a fight we've ever had.

When training for *Strictly* started and we were all rehearsing lots of group numbers, the producers bought in Jason Gilkison and Mandy Moore as choreographers. I'd worked with Mandy on *So You Think You Can Dance* and Jason was the choreographer for *Burn The Floor*. I remember it struck me at that point that it seemed as though we had all arrived at *Strictly* through the same sort of metaphorical sieve – we'd been filtered through *So You Think You Can Dance* and *Burn The Floor* to arrive in the same room together. When you think about it, it makes sense: we all had a desire to perform on television and there are only a limited number of vehicles allowing you to do that. *Burn The Floor* proved to be a great showcase for a lot of my new colleagues and me in allowing us to land the role as a *Strictly* professional.

Of course, I didn't know everyone on the *Strictly* set and, watching my new workmates rehearse, I tried to assess their characters. It struck me how everyone had a definite character and role they were playing within the dynamic of the group. No one was really in the background because everyone had their own little quirky 'thing' to bring to the table.

Anton Du Beke, for example, would always turn up at rehearsals dressed in a suit and tie, even when the rest of us were just in our sweats. He always looked so dapper and he'd come in and give a kiss to all the girls who happened to be in the room (whether they wanted one or not, which they nearly always did!).

Vincent Simone has a little catchphrase and it's the word '*bella*'. He says it all the time and it can mean any number of different things, depending on what he is doing when he says it. So he uses *bella* instead of saying 'hello'. Or it can mean 'look at this!' or it can simply mean that he is really happy at that second. It's just his trademark thing to walk around, constantly saying that word.

Brendan Cole and James Jordan are the jokers in the pack. They have this mischievous banter that goes on between the two of them, but also between them and the rest of the group. They're always trying to play pranks on people, but it's all done in a good-natured way. I remember the first couple of days of rehearsals James kept making witty remarks, centring round me being the new boy. I fired back my own little quips, giving him as good as I was getting, and he would laugh and say, 'I like you!'

I get asked all the time by interviewers and friends if the

Strictly set has the amazing family feel that it seems to have when you watch the programme on television and the answer is yes. Everyone is very supportive of each other.

In the end, it felt completely natural for me to walk straight into rehearsals on my first day and to be immediately accepted into the *Strictly Come Dancing* fold.

By the time the first *Strictly Come Dancing* show of the series is aired to the nation, we dancers know what the celebrity line-up will be (as do the public, as it's usually reported in the newspapers), but not who we will be partnered with for that season.

When you see the presenters Bruce Forsyth and Tess Daly announce who we will be dancing with for that season, live on the very first show, the reaction we have that is captured by the cameras is absolutely genuine. We have no idea what they are about to say. However, the professionals have had to rehearse the group number we perform on that first show. It's an ensemble routine with all the *Strictly* professionals and celebrity contestants, so, not only have we met them, but we have seen them dance a little, too.

It's no secret that all of the professional dancers are hoping at that point that we will be given a celebrity partner who at least has some natural rhythm. That won't necessarily make them any better at ballroom or Latin dancing specifically, which are distinct art forms and different from any other type of dancing, but it will make our lives as their coaches a little easier.

If you think about the experience I had trying to learn other dance styles on the show *So You Think You Can Dance*, you can understand how it works with celebrities of varying levels of skill. For me, learning hip hop and jazz was so difficult after what I was used to, but it certainly helped that I was flexible, fit and strong, and had that foundation to work with and build on. I also knew what it was like to perform in public, which was useful.

It's the same thing with the celebrities on *Strictly Come Dancing*. If you are given someone who has to do some dancing as part of their job – for example, they happen to be a musician who dances on stage – then you know there are certain tools in their kit you can work with. You may even need to help them un-learn the things they already know. Then it becomes just like when I first moved to New York and found that the ballroom technique I had been taught in Siberia wasn't correct and had to start learning almost from scratch with Vibeke and Allan. Sometimes when you're working with a celebrity who has danced before, it's as much about erasing technique they've picked up during their own performance career as about teaching them the ballroom and Latin you will be performing that week.

That's not to say any of us professionals shy away from the challenge of having a celebrity who is perhaps less physically fit or has never really danced before. I have been a *Strictly* professional for two seasons now and for both series I was partnered with two people who were young, flexible and ready to learn. I consider myself very lucky, but, if next time I get a partner who doesn't perhaps fit those same criteria, I am sure I can rise to the challenge. The amount of moves I would be able to do with someone who could not dance at all would be different, but I'd still find a way to make them the best they can be. If someone cannot do the splits, they are never going to be able to do them in the time frame we have to rehearse on *Strictly*, but I can still unlock a lot of other things within them that they didn't know they were able to do.

My first job as dancing mentor is to help my celebrity overcome his or her insecurity. The nature of being a famous person is that they have been known for doing something, be it acting, presenting, singing or athletics, and being the best in their field for a long time. Suddenly, they have to do something completely out of their comfort zone and usually their biggest fear going into the competition is that they will be humiliated in some way. I only have a very short time to gain their trust and to let them know that I would never allow them to look silly on national television. My job is to make them look good and they need to be assured of that.

There's also an intimacy about ballroom and Latin that is really difficult for anyone not used to that kind of dancing to get their head around. Imagine being one of the *Strictly* celebrities, being introduced to your professional partner at one moment and the next having to rehearse holding their hand, or with their hand on your waist and their face only centimetres away from yours! Essentially, you are a stranger but you are going to do things that most people only do with their romantic partners, or their family. For someone who has been dancing for as long as I have, it feels completely normal that I would get into a ballroom hold with a person who is a complete stranger to me but for most people it seems really strange at first.

It's never happened with any of my partners on *Strictly Come Dancing*, but I have seen with some of my students in the past how they have confused the intensity you have to convey when dancing for romantic feeling outside the dance studio. It's easy for me to switch from pretending to be in love with someone on the dance floor (because it fits the character of the dance) to just being the teacher as soon as we step offstage because that's the nature of what I do; it's just the same as it is with acting in a film or play. Yet it's more difficult for a non-performer to separate their emotions on- and offstage. If you just grabbed a random lady off the street and started ballroom dancing with her, she would definitely be thinking, What exactly is going on here?

Whenever I have anyone new to dance with, I always begin slowly, rather than crash right in. I show my students a couple of steps and get them used to doing them on their own. I don't go straight in for a full-on ballroom hold for the reasons stated above. On *Strictly Come Dancing*, I still use that same approach but I have to find ways to accelerate it. You don't have much time to get everything you need to do to pull a performance out of the bag done on *Strictly*. That's why it's so important to establish trust with my celebrity partner early on. A lot of the initial rehearsals are about me working out how far I can push them and how much I can invade their personal space, while letting them know I'm not going to do anything to make them feel uncomfortable.

Strictly Come Dancing is like a crash course through the teaching process: both for me, and the celebrity partner I am working with. What would usually take months, we have to accomplish in a matter of just weeks. It's really all about playing to my celebrity's strengths and working out how to get the best out of them. I notice straight away if my celebrity has a particular natural talent that I can magnify in the routines we present to the judges. They might have naturally good arm movements that create beautiful lines, or a fine hip action, for example. Part of my job as their partner is to devise routines that will showcase their natural talent.

The reason I am sharing all of this with you, the reader, is to convey my belief that anyone can be taught to dance. I think it's really important that anyone reading this book knows that. The reason why the celebrities on *Strictly Come Dancing* look so amazing when they perform and have gained so much skill by the time they get to the final rounds of the show is due to the amount of time they must put in, intensely rehearsing over a short period. For most people, it isn't possible to devote the amount of hours they do to learning a completely new skill, so it could take you longer and you might not reach quite the same level as the celebrities on the show. Having said that, you may have told yourself that you have two left feet, but I don't think anyone is a hopeless case.

You definitely can dance, and, if you think you can't, then you just haven't had the right teacher.

Chapter 28

THE OATH

At the end of August 2011, all the *Strictly Come Dancing* professional dancers got a little two-day vacation from work. The reason for this unexpected holiday was that I had to fly back to Los Angeles and attend to the very important business of becoming an authentic American citizen. There are few things with the power to interrupt the *Strictly* schedule but this had to be one of them. So, I literally flew out to LA for one day and then flew back to London again to carry on rehearsing with *Strictly*. I went out of Britain with a red Russian passport and returned with a blue American one.

My friend Nick, who lives in California, was the most excited out of everyone I knew about the prospect of my becoming an American citizen. He met me at the airport and we attended the ceremony together.

What happens during the citizenship ceremony differs from state to state. Mine took place in this huge room in Los

Angeles, where I'd been living prior to coming over to London. There must have been around 3,000 people in that room from all over the world, all waiting to become official citizens of the United States.

I remember laughing as I thought about how the room showed you can literally turn anything into an opportunity to sell tacky products. As we walked through the hall, all these stalls were selling things like flowers, or little teddy bears with the date that you became an American on them. You could get a photograph taken, or buy a book with the date on it and there were also people selling frames and covers for your certificate of citizenship. I didn't buy anything but I walked around taking photos of myself with all the various bits of merchandise for sale. I thought it was really funny that, during a ceremony to become an American, everything was 'made in China'.

After all 3,000 or so of us were seated, some officials came out and talked to us about what it means to be an American. After that, it was time for us to say the oath from the U.S. Department of Homeland Security that would make it all legal. The officials would say the words one sentence at a time and then we would all repeat them back as a group.

You say, 'I hereby declare, on oath, that I absolutely and entirely renounce and abjure all allegiance and fidelity to any foreign prince, potentate, state, or sovereignty of whom or which I have heretofore been a subject or citizen; that I will support and defend the Constitution and laws of the United States of America against all enemies, foreign and domestic; that I will bear true faith and allegiance to the same; that I will bear arms on behalf of the United States when required by law; that I will perform noncombatant service in the Armed Forces of the United States when required by the law; that I will perform work of national importance under civilian direction when required by the law; and that I take this obligation freely without any mental reservation or purpose of evasion; so help me God'.

Then we all sang our new National Anthem, 'The Star-Spangled Banner'.

I felt very proud to have finally become a proper US citizen. It had been 11 years since I left Russia. I don't know how you are supposed to feel if you are a Russian, or a British person, but I did know in my gut that I felt like an American. As soon as I had stepped onto US soil, I'd felt it was my spiritual home. Everything about the place had felt good to me. I soon discovered that the mentality of the people matched mine. The American nation share an attitude about how things should be done and it was exactly how I liked them to be done.

For a long time in my mind, America had been where I belonged, and now it had been made official.

Chapter 29

CHELSEE

One of the celebrities I had identified as someone with some natural dance ability when we were rehearsing the group routines was Chelsee Healey.

During that first *Strictly* group number, I had to dance a little with Chelsee as well as four of the other female contestants – Anita Dobson, Edwina Curry, Holly Valance and Nancy Dell'Olio. I noticed when dancing with Chelsee that she had great arm movements. She was able to create really nice lines when she moved her arms and seemed to be doing it instinctually, without being told to. So, I was really happy when, during the first live *Strictly Come Dancing* show of 2011, it was announced that Chelsee would be my partner for that season.

Chelsee was part of the cast of a really popular British television show called *Waterloo Road*, which is filmed up in Manchester. Every day, I had to travel the 200 miles from my new home in London to where she was based in Manchester and meet her after she finished work so we could practise our routines. Chelsee was so incredibly busy during that time. She was picked up at around 6am to go to the *Waterloo Road* set and she'd finish filming around 12 hours later, at 6pm. Then she'd come to the gym space that was hired out for our rehearsals and spend two or three hours every day with me.

From the very first day we began rehearsing, Chelsee kept talking about not wanting to feel 'daft'. I hadn't heard that word before but realised after a while it meant 'silly' and therefore it was really important to her how she was perceived by the viewing public.

Chelsee had given a quote during an interview shown as a VT (or 'video trailer' – one of the little videos *Strictly* shows of the contestants rehearsing before their live performance) on the first show and said that she was 'single and ready to mingle'. Afterwards, she told me it was one of the things that made her feel 'daft' because then of course there was all this expectation from the press and the viewers at home that something romantic was going to happen between Chelsee and her professional partner, who turned out to be me. I was not single at that time but I hadn't talked about my relationship in the press or any sort of public forum because that's just not the type of thing I tend to do. I don't want to expose the people I care about to any kind of unwelcome scrutiny. So, as far as anyone knew, I was available and Chelsee was 'single and ready to mingle', which created this buzz around what was going on, or *might* go on, between the two of us.

I told her not to worry about that and just to focus on the dance, which was the most important thing.

I remember thinking after getting to know Chelsee a little

that being famous had not spoiled her in any way. She is a very straightforward person and her intentions are genuine. I think the expression is 'what you see is what you get'! She didn't seem to have an agenda for going on the show, other than wanting to learn how to dance. I also recall thinking that Chelsee was very sweet and occasionally a little naïve. She once asked Brendan, if he was from New Zealand, how come he spoke such good English. Little things like that would make me chuckle.

I quickly discovered that, as a dancer, Chelsee is naturally more Latin orientated than ballroom. That made sense. She was only 23 years old at that time and was a young woman who liked to party a lot. When you see the way people dance in nightclubs now, the way it is currently fashionable to dance, that 'shake your booty' thing is a lot closer to Latin than ballroom.

For the first *Strictly* show and the group performance, Chelsee was wearing a really revealing dress. She has, by her own admission, a surgically enhanced bust and the dress showed a lot of cleavage, as well as leg. Her huge hair was helped by lots of hair extensions and she looked like this sexy lioness. So, the initial image of Chelsee, with which the viewers had been presented, plus her natural propensity for Latin dancing, meant that it was a challenge for me when we were told that our first dance together would be a waltz. The waltz is all about elegance, class and sophistication. It's very romantic, with no room for sexy booty shaking within the routine!

From that point on, it became my goal to change not only the audience's perspective on Chelsee but also the way that she saw herself. I wanted her to realise that she could be the kind of graceful and elegant dancer she needed to be in order to perform the waltz. I knew the demographic who watch *Strictly* tend to be in their thirties and above, all the way up to pensioners. I figured they might take a more conservative view of things than, say, the audience who watched *So You Think You Can Dance*, who tended to be people in their teens and twenties. I wanted the audience to warm to Chelsee and to see that she was more than just this scantily clad wild thing they had caught a glimpse of so far.

The first thing I did was talk to *Strictly's* costume department so that we could work together to find some really classy pieces for Chelsee to wear during the series.

Later in the competition, Chelsee and I did a VT, where we re-enacted a scene from *My Fair Lady*, a musical about a Professor Henry Higgins who teaches a young woman (played by Audrey Hepburn) how to be a sophisticated lady. So, by using that as a hook, the audience could quickly grasp what it was Chelsee and I were trying to work towards.

It was as much about Chelsee believing she could do it as it was about the audience's perception of her, though. Slowly, over the two weeks we practised our first routine. I watched Chelsee transform into someone who had faith in the idea that she could perform a waltz.

This transformation continued right up into week four of the competition, when we performed a quickstep. We had a big band in the studio and we danced the routine to a lyric-less version of the song 'Sing Sing Sing (With A Swing)', which is a really famous old show tune. I wanted the dance to have a very authentic feel to it and to make the audience nostalgic for a time when quickstep would have been performed with the big band playing. The story we conveyed with the dance was that Chelsee was an air stewardess and I was a passenger who had lost my ticket. By the end of the dance, she had found my ticket for me, which was in my pocket.

That was the first time Chelsee had her hair all slicked back into a chignon. She looked very proper and totally different to when she had the huge mane of hair before. The quickstep represented the middle ground we'd been able to carve between making Chelsee into a very elegant performer, but also acknowledging that she is a young woman who wants to have fun. The dance is smooth and graceful but also fast paced so it's a combination of sophistication and youth, which was exactly the point that Chelsee had reached on her personal journey by then.

The week when we performed the air stewardess routine marked a huge surge in Chelsee's confidence and that came across in the performance. The *Strictly* judges all gave us a score of nine for that routine, whereas in the previous weeks we'd been getting sevens and eights.

By that stage, the relationship between Chelsee and me had developed into something like that of a big brother and his little sister. I remember she was very typical of people her age in that whenever I would give her even a second's break in the studio she would be straight onto her phone, checking her Twitter feed. She'd do it even if I paused for one minute to think about a change in choreography. It was my job to keep her focused so I'd say, 'Right, come on, Chelsee, we have to keep dancing now,' and she'd do that thing people do where she'd walk towards me and be talking to me but still looking at her phone at the same time! There were a couple of occasions when I had to confiscate her phone so we could do what we needed to do. I'd only take the phone for a few minutes before giving it back, but it was enough to make the point.

I've never really had much desire to go on any social media. I do have a Facebook and Twitter account and very occasionally I'll log on to read a message someone has sent me. I'll see my news feed and know what everyone I know has been getting up to and think, Oh look, they are alive and doing things! Fantastic! That's really the extent of my interest, though. I have never felt that I would like to go on Twitter and let the world know what I'm doing at that moment or my opinion on certain things. People tell me social media is good for business but, the way I see it, business has been good without it.

Having said that, I could understand what was attracting Chelsee to social media websites. Simply because I didn't have the desire to socially network myself didn't mean that I couldn't see it was important to her. I think, if Chelsee hadn't had that means of chatting with her friends and the outside world, it would have been really easy for her to feel isolated at that time. She was a young woman who was spending all day on set and all evening rehearsing with me. Her social life during that time was suffering as a result so she needed that little window into what was happening outside.

There were a couple of examples like that where teaching Chelsee was about my having to be sensitive and not apply my own standards to her. In the very beginning of our time together, there was an occasion in the studio when I pushed her too hard and I learned not to do it again. We weren't getting this one part of the dance we were rehearsing absolutely right and I kept going over it again and again, thinking if we did it often enough then eventually we'd nail it. Chelsee was getting really frustrated with herself and she ended up storming out of the studio. She came back about two minutes later and apologised but I realised at that point how much pressure she was under and that I must always be mindful of that.

In the end, all of our hard work paid off because Chelsee and I made it to the final round of *Strictly Come Dancing*. We danced four dances for the last show but my favourite was the rumba. I think that was probably the best Chelsee ever danced. She showcased a lot of the technique she had learned over the weeks, which you have to be able to do in the slower dances, and throughout she was very emotional in the character she was portraying.

That was the moment when I looked at her and thought, I have done a good job. You are a proper dancer, now!

Even though Chelsee was given the runner-up position in season nine of *Strictly* she still managed to get one of the show's coveted glitter ball trophies. She was given the glitter ball for a different challenge that we undertook together for the charity Sport Relief.

Harry Judd and his partner, Aliona, as well as Chelsee and me were asked to perform a live televised competitive ballroom dance underwater on 23 March 2012. The challenge took place at Pinewood Studios, famous for having been the venue for lots of movies with underwater scenes, including *James Bond* and *Pirates Of The Caribbean*. On arrival, we saw that we would be dancing in a huge tank, which must have been around six metres deep, with a dance floor at the bottom. The tank was cleaned with UV lights, so they did not have to use chlorine and there were windows at the side so that people could see in.

This challenge was not so much about the dancing as the diving. Dancing underwater is fantastic because you are given a different level at which to perform your movements. Everything becomes less flat when you are no longer restricted by gravity. I was really excited by the prospect of the actual routine we would be performing. Yet, learning how to breathe and keep ourselves at the bottom of the tank would prove taxing – for me, physically and psychologically for Chelsee.

After being given small air tanks that would allow us to breathe underwater for perhaps six or seven minutes, we were instructed in how to use them and what to do if the tank was faulty or not working properly for whatever reason.

In the original routine I devised with Chelsee, I had to dive from the top of the tank down onto the dance floor, right at the beginning. I was going from the surface of the water to six metres deep in a matter of seconds. After rehearsing that time and time again, I was in a lot of pain. The change in pressure meant my eyes were bloodshot and streaming, and my ears and all the joints in my body were hurting. In the end, I could not do that part of the dance because it was simply hurting too much.

Chelsee, meanwhile, was struggling with the psychological aspects of having to go that deep underwater and stay there for the performance. While Harry and Aliona happily got to grips with the diving bit and were rehearsing their routine next to us, Chelsee had to be gently coaxed to go down to the dance floor for a few seconds before coming up again in a state of total panic.

I spent a lot of time sitting at the bottom of the tank like a little frog, waiting for Chelsee to come down and join me. The diving instructors taught me how to blow rings in the water, like smoke rings, while I was down there, waiting. That was a lot of fun. It was the strangest sensation, though – being under-water in a full ballroom dancing costume, especially when we came out of the water and our clothes were so heavy and sticking to us. I remember thinking, This doesn't feel right. I never sweat so much during a performance that my clothes are in that state so it was completely alien to me!

I have to give Chelsee props for the fact that she never gave up. She kept on trying to get down to the bottom of the tank and, eventually, we were able to go through and practise our routine just once from start to finish before it was time for the live performance.

Mostly because they had far more time to rehearse, I thought that Harry and Aliona's routine was more well executed and closer to what it should have been. However, despite this, we were given identical scores, and head judge Len Goodman, who had the deciding vote, then chose us as the winners. Len felt that Chelsee was doing more underwater because she was the female dancer, so her part of the dance involved a lot more movement.

I was very proud of Chelsee in that moment. She had conquered her fear and been declared a champion, after all.

Chapter 30

BODY IMAGE

After season one of *Strictly Come Dancing* finished and we'd completed the *Strictly Live Tour*, I began touring Britain with my professional partner from the series, Katya Virshilas.

The show was now in its second season in 2012, during which we performed high-intensity, passionate and intricate numbers. To perform in this way 40 or 50 times every night takes so much stamina and endurance and we are always injuring ourselves in some way. While performing that first tour, Katya somehow managed to dislocate her ribs. On a couple of occasions we'd have to make an emergency call to a physiotherapist to come backstage and pop her ribs back in so she could go back on and do the show. I can see how to a non-dancer this would seem really extreme, but this is what we have to do as dancers for the 'show to go on'. That's why we need the best physiotherapists to make it as safe and as effective as possible. During rehearsals for the second tour, which we're actually performing at various locations as I write this book, Katya broke her finger and I have a problem with my shoulder popping out.

The issue with my shoulder actually dates back to my days dancing with *Burn The Floor* on Broadway. I was warming up before the show using one of those stretchy, elastic exercise bands and one of my fellow cast members told me that I wasn't doing it right and pushed down on my shoulder as I was stretching. For two weeks after that, my left shoulder wouldn't work properly; I couldn't even hold my partner in the traditional way. We are supposed to lead with our left arm but I had to improvise and lead with my right until the pain subsided. Ever since then, I have felt as if my shoulder isn't quite in the right place.

There was never any question of my taking a break from *Burn The Floor* while my shoulder got better. We had eight shows per week at that point and they had to somehow get danced! That's pretty typical of the mentality you build throughout a dancing career. When you are a dancer, you use your body as the tool of your trade. Because you use it so much, inevitably it gets worn down. You get to a stage where you are used to having some level of pain or discomfort at any given moment but it never occurs to you to stop what you are doing.

I was fortunate because my injury was not as serious as Katya's. There were times when we would be dancing together when I could feel that she was just this tight ball of tension and clenched muscle because she was in so much pain. On those occasions, she would be going through the motions of the dance but she couldn't even smile.

Luckily, we have found an incredible physiotherapist named Colin, who we always call when a body emergency arises on tour. Unlike a lot of the doctors I have seen throughout my career, he understands the cause and symptoms of pain are not one and the same. For example, if you have a pain in your knee, it does not mean that the issue is emanating from your knee. The problem could be somewhere else entirely within your body but the end result is that it is pulling at your kneecap and causing you pain in that area. Colin works by finding the root of the problem.

Katya and I have been very lucky to find Colin. He has minimised the amount of discomfort we feel when having to deal with the physical demands of touring.

Other than those sorts of injuries, I can't say that my body ever bothers me that much. I'm often asked whether being a dancer has affected how I feel about my physique, whether it has made me more conscious of it, or more vain. The entertainment business has a reputation for being full of insecurity and narcissism, so I guess it's a valid question, even though I'm not really like that.

Unlike some of the other professional dancers on *Strictly Come Dancing*, I don't even get a spray tan. I do like to have a tan and, by the time the series starts, I've usually spent a few weeks back in Los Angeles so I will have picked up a bit of sun. Halfway through the series that fades and I'm back to being a pale Russian boy! I know everyone looks better with a tan on screen but I don't like the feel of the fake stuff. The skin is the biggest organ in the body and I've always felt that it needs to be able to breathe in order to be healthy.

Whenever I have thought about my body, it's always in

relation to what it can do, rather than how it looks. I am by nature a very competitive person; I always see my main competition as being my previous self – I want to push myself a little harder each day. So the only time I would ever get frustrated with my body would be if it could not do an activity that I needed, or wanted it to do.

I started dancing at a very young age so I was plunged straight into an environment where I was expected to compete and keep up with a group, some of whom were much older than me. I remember when I first started dancing as part of a studio, I'd look at the older kids, who'd be able to do our high-intensity warm-up easily, without even getting out of breath, because they'd been doing it for so long. I'd be struggling and have a stitch but I was determined not to show it and to act like it was just as easy for me as it was for them.

I carried this attitude through the whole time I was learning and growing as a dancer. After five minutes of doing jive, which is pretty much the most intense and energetic dance you can do, I'd always try to walk off the dance floor in a casual way, as if nothing had happened.

Whatever level you reach, rehearsals are always very intense and athletic – you have to push yourself hard to develop your craft. That's why it often seems like the celebrity contestants on *Strictly Come Dancing* change body shape so drastically in the first couple of weeks; most people aren't used to doing that level of activity.

At my studio back in Siberia, we would always begin with a 90-minute warm-up to fast-paced music. At the end, we'd literally be standing in a puddle of our own sweat. That was before we had even started to properly dance!

I remember one time my Siberian coach, Irina, went to England and saw a particular way they used to rotate the dancers when rehearsing in the Simley London studio for the famous annual Blackpool competition. Blackpool Dance Festival is a Mecca for ballroom dancers, being one of the most prestigious competitions in the world. Thousands of couples flock there every year. At Simley, the dance floor itself is quite small so they'd have to take it in turns to rehearse. The floor took about 20 couples at any one time. Those couples would make up one 'heat'. Later, I experienced this for myself when I came over for the Blackpool competition. While waiting for your heat, you simply stand at the side of the dance floor watching the other couples and trying to work out who your fiercest competition is.

For some reason, Irina decided that we should apply the Simley system to our studio in Russia, even though there was room for everyone to dance at the same time. She liked their way of doing things – I think maybe she wanted to test us. Because there were only a limited number of dancers, 'rotating' in our studio in reality meant having to dance one dance six times, then all the other dances once and so on. So we'd dance the cha-cha-cha six times, then one samba, one jive, one paso doble and one rumba. Then it would be six sambas, followed by the rest. We'd dance like that for three hours at a time, non-stop.

Afterwards, some of the other kids would be lying on the floor as though they were dead – they were so exhausted. I'd always try to pretend that I wasn't tired. For me, it was a matter of pride that I could do it.

As it turned out, dancing with a Simley-style rotation prepared me really well for some of the other professional competitions I undertook later in life. Sometimes you'd have to dance 10 rounds in a row, so only the fittest would survive. In such contests, it stops being about who is the best dancer technically, and is more about who has the most stamina. Some couples were clearly the best dancers for two or three rounds but they just couldn't go the distance.

Some of the other people I trained with at the studio didn't take our warm-ups and training exercises as seriously as I did and, looking back, they never fared as well in the competitions. My thirst to always excel myself and to beat my last record, to always push my body to its limits, has really served me well over the years, although I might not have appreciated it at the time.

From a very early age, we built muscles and did everything we could to maintain them. We dancers didn't like to spent time in physical education lessons at boarding school because we knew we would be the fastest and the strongest, so it seemed just too easy. Instead, we'd ask to be excluded so we could spend more time doing the physical activities that did challenge us and allowed us to compete on a level with each other.

I remember at the end of each school semester we'd have a fitness assessment with push-ups, pull-ups and a timed sprint. It was always a breeze for the dancers. One time, our teacher said to us, 'You have to do something, some kind of competition or sports activity that's not dancing, so that I can give you a grade.'

We were asked to compete on behalf of the school in a ski run. Because we were healthy and athletic, it was assumed we would be able to do it, despite the fact that none of us had any skiing experience at all. Also, we didn't have any of the proper attire or equipment; we just turned up in whatever we happened to be wearing. We didn't have proper skis or ski boots, just our normal shoes held to a vaguely ski-shaped plank by a small loop of string.

We didn't really try that hard to win the competition – we even had a little rest in the middle of the ski run! Of course, we hadn't been told to win, just to take part so that we could get a grade and pass that year of school, so it didn't seem too important to us. In the end, we did quite well in the league table of those who were competing that day; I remember that we were somewhere in the middle.

I think that clearly being okay at skiing, even though we were wearing normal clothes, had no experience and didn't even try, taught us that dancing is a great preparation for any kind of sport. It builds your core muscles and fitness level, giving you a foundation, which means you can turn your hand to pretty much anything.

So you can see that dancing really is one of the best ways to work out. Later on in my career, though, dancing became less of a workout and more like meditation. I tried yoga and real meditation a few times and now I recognise that I get the same feelings when I dance. Dancing allows me to be in tune with myself; I have a total awareness in my body and a focus in my mind.

When I dance, it's almost like the traditional roles of my mind and body are swapped; I'm thinking with my body and moving with my mind. Occasionally, I'll have something akin to an out-of-body experience. It's as if I'm observing myself dancing. I don't feel as if I have control over what I am doing, everything happens on an instinctual level. If you do something often enough, it becomes automatic and so it is with the steps in the dances I know so well. My brain becomes like my body's manager – it is overseeing the process, making sure that every-thing is working in harmony.

Dancers always have the worst feet in the world to look at. It's partly because we're wearing really tight shoes all the time. Our shoes have to be tied tight to make our feet aerodynamic and streamlined so the shoe becomes almost like a second skin, conforming exactly to the line of the foot. It's also because we're constantly in motion. We develop calluses, bruises and blisters all over our feet.

I never want to show my feet to anyone, mainly because I know what the reaction will be. They always say, 'Oh, Pasha! You should take better care of yourself!' What they don't realise is that I *need* those calluses – they are there to protect my feet from everything I put them through on a day-to-day basis. It's the same thing with musicians who play the guitar – when they first start playing, the strings hurt their fingers, then they develop hard skin on the ends of their fingertips which means it doesn't hurt any more. This is what allows them to develop their craft.

Even though I don't have any hang ups about how my body looks, I have seen it in other dancers, and particularly in the female ones I have worked with over the years. Back in the studios, I remember always hearing the girl dancers talk about how they needed to lose more weight – they always seemed to be on a diet. It was crazy because you need to eat a lot in order to do all the physical activity required to train, but they were never taking in enough energy.

Us guys didn't, as far as I was aware, have the same problems. Certainly not me, I know. My whole life, I have eaten a lot because I've needed the energy to do what I do for a living. As

I've become slightly older, I've noticed that I gain weight really fast when I stop dancing because I don't tend to eat any less during that time. It didn't used to happen when I was younger and had the crazy metabolism of someone who could eat whatever he wanted. I guess I might need to keep an eye on that in the future. Mostly, though, I'm just grateful to be here. Especially since the health scare I had in New York City, I've realised the most important thing is to be alive, and how lucky I am that my body allows me to do what I love most.

Chapter 31

KIMBERLEY

On the first series I was involved with *Strictly Come Dancing*, which was series nine of the show, the very first routine I performed with Chelsee Healey we danced to a song called 'See The Day' by Girls Aloud. So, it felt like it might be fate when, after I was invited back to perform in series 10, I was partnered with Kimberley Walsh, who at the time just happened to be a member of the band Girls Aloud. (Incidentally, my first dance with Kimberley was to a track by Rihanna so I always joke that she will be my celebrity partner on the next series of the show!)

This time around, I'd rented a different flat in Notting Hill. I loved the idea of living there, I'm not sure why – maybe because of the movie of the same name. It just seemed significant to me at the time. It was a Thursday when I moved into my new place and, on Friday, I came out onto the street and saw all the shop owners on Westbourne Grove boarding up their windows. 'Did they declare a war and no one told me?' I asked, eager to find out what was going on.

They laughed and explained that it was the weekend of the famous Notting Hill Carnival, which celebrates Caribbean culture and attracts people from all over the world, who come to the streets to dance and enjoy music and traditional food. From that morning to the early hours of the next, there were stampedes of crowds walking right past my window. Thousands upon thousands of people must have gone by, playing music, singing and shouting. There was no way I could do anything indoors so I decided to take a walk around the block, but it took me an hour because everywhere was so congested, so I just had to come back and listen to all the noise. That was the first day I had to 'rest' in my new home!

I still live in that same apartment I'm describing. It's near Portobello Market, which is really cool but, again, very noisy. I've just about got used to all the noise now and I don't even hear it. In particular, there is a guy who plays cello on the corner next to my house. He plays the same songs over and over again for the tourists and at first it would drive me insane, but now it doesn't even register so I guess I've become accustomed to London.

When I first found my flat, I was hoping I'd get a celebrity partner this time around who actually lived in London and finally get the chance to explore the city. As luck would have it, I was paired with Kimberley, who lives in London, but I still haven't managed to do that exploring! I always seem to be too busy and not have the time.

Once *Strictly Come Dancing* starts, it's like a machine that doesn't stop. I am always thinking about the next piece of music or choreography, or costumes for the next performance. Even on the one day off we are given each week, I would find myself planning rehearsals the next day so I would come to my celebrity fully prepared. I have to say that I like it that way – I enjoy immersing myself in a project. If I allow myself to rest when I'm working, it's always that much tougher to get back into 'dance mode' the next day, so it's better just to keep on ploughing through, even if it means I'm exhausted by the time the project comes to an end.

Again, the first time I met Kimberley was when we all rehearsed the group routine in August 2012, before the first *Strictly* show of the series. For some reason, the producers had all of the celebrities come in wearing masks, printed with Bruce Forsyth's face on them. About a week before, the *Sun* newspaper had printed a list of all the contestants that series, so we knew who they were despite the masks.

I immediately identified Kimberley, Denise van Outen and Dani Harmer as being the strongest female contestants that year and hoped I would be paired with one of them. For some reason, I had a kind of instinct about who my partner would be this time around and I felt that it would be Kimberley. It was nothing but a hunch, but that's why, when you see my reaction to the announcement on camera, I don't seem all that surprised.

From the very beginning, Kimberley struck me as a very calm and down-to-earth sort of person. As we got to know each other, I found out that our characters are actually quite similar: we are both perfectionists who are focused on the goal in front of us, but neither of us is prone to doing so by screaming and shouting about it.

Kimberley and I were able to rehearse for a lot more hours

each week than I had been able to with Chelsee. Even though Kimberley had commitments with Girls Aloud, as well as her own solo album coming out, she was able to be a lot more flexible and move things around so that we could have a good block of time in the studio together.

I found out very early on that Kimberley is not someone who is afraid of hard work. She really wanted to learn the proper technique for each arm movement or footstep and she was never satisfied until she had it absolutely right. During the rehearsal process, I used this to my advantage. I would use reverse psychology on her by saying, 'Well, that looks all right. It's not perfect, but we can practise more tomorrow. Let's finish for the day,' knowing she would insist on staying in the studio and rehearsing until whatever we were doing was perfect.

Although the perfectionist element of Kimberley's nature was an advantage in rehearsals, it would sometimes hinder her in performance because she'd have a last-minute crisis of confidence. As we were about to take the stage for our first performance together on *Strictly*, I suddenly saw this side to her that I'd never encountered before. She was really freaking out about how the dance would be perceived and thinking of all the things that might go wrong.

This became a theme for all of our live performances during the series, right up to week 10. Kimberley would be fine in rehearsals but then, when we had to do that walk down the stairs and onto the *Strictly* stage, she started to get really stressed and began to shake like a leaf on a tree in autumn. After week ten, she found some confidence, but up until that point I had to be a rock for her and make her realise that she could do the performance and everything would be okay.

I got into the habit of giving Kimberley a little pep talk each week before our performance. All her anxiety seemed to build up into that moment just before the music starts. Luckily, coming from a performance background, she knew that once the music started it was show time and she always managed to pull it off, week after week.

Every show, the scores Kimberley and I had been getting from the *Strictly* judges were getting higher and higher, until week six when we suddenly found ourselves in the bottom two. Looking back, I have no idea why that happened. We had danced a Viennese waltz and, as far as I was concerned, it was the best Kimberley had ever performed. She danced beautifully and was so in character, it was as though no one else existed but the two of us on the dance floor. You know someone is really lost in a dance when they forget about a live studio audience, cameras and millions of viewers at home! Yet, for some reason, we didn't get the votes we needed to automatically go through to the next round.

The way the results are announced on *Strictly*, each couple stands in a circle of light and then, if it is announced that they are proceeding to the next week, the light goes out until only three are left switched on. Then the bottom two couples have their lights turned red. When you talk to the celebrity contestants, they will tell you that standing in that circle of light, waiting to see if their light will turn red is the most stressful part of the show. None of them wants to go home. The whole atmosphere of *Strictly* is amazing and they get used to it so quickly that they never want it to end.

Whether it was Chelsee and me or Kimberley and me standing there, I could feel how nervous they were at that point in the show. They both used to squeeze my hand so hard, as if they were clinging onto a cliff face about to drop. Luckily, Chelsee never found herself having to face the dance-off among the bottom two, but in this particular week, week six, Kimberley did.

The judges chose to give Kimberley and me another shot and send the other couple, Fern Britton and her partner Artem, home. I already knew from my time on *So You Think You Can Dance* how that experience of being saved felt and I wondered whether Kimberley would let it knock her confidence, or if she would come to rehearsals the next day stronger and more determined. I was delighted when it was the latter. Kimberley told me she was going to do whatever it took not to find herself in the bottom two again.

After that Viennese waltz, Kimberley let go of that careful side of her and began diving into all the dance routines we were performing with passion and vigour. One of my favourites was when we performed a tango to 'When Doves Cry' by Prince, but there were lots of memorable dances.

In week 10, we performed a cha-cha-cha and tango fusion to 'It's Raining Men' and received the first perfect score of 40 of that series. After that, we stayed at the top of the leader board. I remember thinking it was the perfect way round; before that day, we'd been getting scores of sevens, eights and nines but we didn't peak too soon and got tens in the final stretch of the competition. It's a little like running a marathon: if you are in the lead from the outset, then it's unlikely you will be by the time you cross the finish line.

Again, Kimberley and I found ourselves in the runner-up position, just as Chelsee and I had in series nine. I couldn't have been prouder of Kimberley if she had actually won. She'd come so far since being the girl who doubted her abilities in the initial weeks.

Exactly like when Chelsee had said, 'I'm single and ready to mingle,' there was some speculation in the press about whether or not a romance was developing between Kimberley and me. Again, I was not single myself and this time neither was Kimberley so that kind of relationship was just never on the cards for the two of us.

I guess, when you put any two young people together and they are coming out and dancing these romantic or sexy routines, people are going to read more into it. It's not always without foundation, either. There are lots of celebrities and professional dancers on *Strictly* (and in other dancing shows too) that have gone on to become girlfriend and boyfriend. Trying to work out which couples will emerge before it's officially announced is all part of the theatre of such television shows but I can definitely confirm that, in the case of my celebrity partners, the rumours had no truth in them at all.

What did develop between Kimberley and me was a friendship that has endured to this day. I feel that she has taught me as much as I was able to teach her during our time dancing together. Kimberley has an extraordinary integrity and treats everyone with equal respect, even though she is one of Britain's most successful pop stars.

During our time dancing together on *Strictly*, I went to meet Kimberley for rehearsals at the place where she was filming the music video for her cover of the song 'One Day I'll Fly Away'. Since I was there anyway, the producers asked if I'd like to do a little choreography and maybe appear in the video. I was happy to step in. The result was a beautiful story in which Kimberley is a lonely ballerina singing about her imaginary lover, who is played by me. I appear for just a few seconds in the video alongside Kimberley, but she dances throughout it.

I think anyone who watches 'One Day I'll Fly Away' can see that, after all the hard work she put into transforming herself into a dancer, Kimberley was able to accomplish exactly that.

Chapter 32

'KEEP DANCING!'

What life has taught me is that, despite our desire always to be in control of things, human beings are playing a game that it is impossible to lose. Whatever happens, there are always so many different ways you can look at things. You can see events as obstacles, or as opportunities. Ultimately, I believe that whatever life has in store is for the best: it's up to me to be flexible enough in my view to see it that way.

Looking back over my life during the course of writing this book, I've noticed how everything fitted together, like pieces of a puzzle, in a way that I could never have seen at the time. There was no 'turning point' or 'life-changing moment' (unless you count my birth. *That* was pretty huge for me!). It all had to happen, every single last bit of it, in order for me to be where I am today.

I don't know what to expect or what's around the corner. I don't have a plan, other than to dance for as long as I can in whatever capacity I can, because it's the only thing I know that I love to do, at this point.

It's like Bruce Forsyth says at the end of every *Strictly Come Dancing* show. My plan is to keep dancing...